BRIGHT WINGS TO FLY

BRIGHT WINGS TO FLY

AN APPALACHIAN FAMILY
IN THE CIVIL WAR

BRUCE HOPKINS

WIND PUBLICATIONS

International Standard Book Number 1893239551
Library of Congress Control Number   2006921138

First edition

Front Cover — "On the Big Sandy" by Jerry Miller

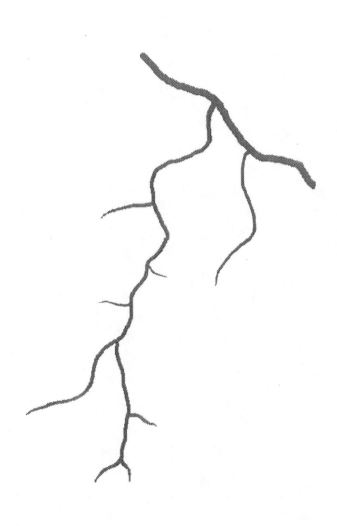

Prologue: July 1904

*O*nly *a few people climbed the narrow, twisting mountain road up to the old man's cabin that night, for in truth few people on Greasy Creek knew he was still alive when the word came and perhaps still fewer cared. It was not easy to be friend or family to Elisha Hopkins in his final years. Even the urchins of the creek had tired of throwing stones at his cabin to provoke his fury, since now there was none; the old man no longer stormed off the porch to rage at them in fearsome, blasphemous oaths and instead merely sat and glared at their indiscretions. When he declined even that response, the boys found no peril in their actions and lost interest in favor of other prey.*

Nor were there Indians among the procession, but there were no Indians on Greasy Creek anymore. They would have come, had they been there, for they were his friends. For half a century, until he quit making whiskey from it, he was the best customer for their honey, but that was not the true reason for their friendship. Of all the people on Greasy Creek, he knew them best. He had hunted with them, farmed and fished with them, listened attentively when the elders spoke, and learned their legends. On summer nights, he would sit around their campfires and watch the bright sparks lift up into the sky, lunging for the stars like souls straining for heaven, and flickering out, their earthly fire extinguished, when they arrived at the Gate. And so many times, he stayed up all night beside open graves, chanting with them to frighten away evil spirits, until daylight, when he would help them bury their dead.

They would have come, had they been there, for they owed him that.

Perhaps he was of their blood somehow, with his dark eyes, and his hair still hinting of darkness even into his ninth decade. And it was said he had taken an Indian bride, one of four he had, but if he ever admitted he was of the People, no one could recall him speaking of it. But he would not speak of the past at all, and no one on Greasy Creek spoke of the old days anymore. Those who could remember, those like him who came to Old Greasy when it and they were young, were equally reticent. If the topic were broached, they would change the subject or pretend they had not heard the question. There was little left of the place Greasy Creek once was, the place Elisha knew a lifetime ago.

Even the great trees were gone and the hillsides nearly bare, except for the rotting stumps where a man could stretch out without his legs falling off the side. They were like huge flat gravestones covering the tombs of giants, but there was no honor to these markers, and the giants themselves were nearly forgotten.

From down in the valley, the lights in his cabin could easily be seen on top of Ripley Knob. The pilgrims making their way up the mountain path would rarely lose sight of the lanterns his family hung outside as beacons. Ten years before that warm July night, that would not have been possible, for the trees, the giant yellow poplars that a squad of Confederate riflemen could have hidden behind and sometimes did, would have choked the light. But now the scrub was up barely chest high, and only the youngest children of the creek would live to see a forest return.

That was why the Indians left. It was true they had been pushed further and further into the hollows and had fewer places to live because only a small number of them had perfected deeds to their lands. But they could have adapted; they had before, even before the awful year of 1838, before there was no penalty to being the People. Even afterward, with their assumption of English names and English ways, like schools and churches, they could have stayed, and they would still have been the People, if only in their deepest heart, the heart that Elisha knew.

But the great trees were gone, cut down and hauled away, and there was no place left for the gods to live, no place for the People to join them when they died, no sanctuary for the spirits that would

2

otherwise wander the earth forever. When they saw what remained, they knew they could no longer live in such a soulless place.

Some said they went to Oklahoma where they had kin; letters came from there and the Indians would ask the scribes of Greasy Creek to read them and reply. But the letters continued long after they disappeared and the pile of uncollected mail grew until their senders, weary from lack of response, quit writing altogether.

Others thought the Indians had gone back to North Carolina, an even more distant memory to the People, to the place where they once lived and where the great trees yet stood. But wherever they went, they would have said goodbye to Elisha; if they spoke to anyone it would have been him, but he would not say so. They left in the night, leaving nothing in their cabins but a few sprigs of evergreen above the open doorways and a few smooth pebbles on the cold hearths, and no one ever saw them again.

Outside Elisha's cabin the wake had already begun, although the old man still breathed raggedly, and the men passed bottles between them, waiting for the women to tell them it was over. What they drank was not as good as the amber liquid Elisha was famous for, but how could it be? A vice president of the United States once declared Elisha's whiskey to be the finest he had ever tasted, and he had tasted plenty, but he was gone too. Some said there was a bottle left somewhere on the creek, hidden in a loft for a special occasion or buried under a marker tree like pirate's loot and infinitely more precious. If it existed, no one would have revealed its location; it would have been secreted from thieves who would not have appreciated its magic, would not have understood what it meant to taste nectar worthy of the gods. But no one really believed such a relic survived. They knew no one could resist Elisha's whiskey, just as few women could resist his charm; they would have fought for it like sinners falling into the Pit, giving up a final glimpse of all they had lost in their desperation. That night on the mountain, it was more Elisha's whiskey they mourned than the man, but they toasted both with the rude liquor they brought with them. They had long ago learned to make do with what they had.

The hardy women who climbed the mountain behind their men brought food and piled it onto the table or the sideboard or the cast iron stove that was kept warm for coffee in spite of the July heat.

3

Elisha had laboriously hauled that stove up the hill with his team twenty-five years before, when even as an old man he had the strength to claim an extended youth and a fourth bride. But after two decades of cooking food for the family and heating their bodies in winter, it was abandoned and sat there for years, unused and rusting, until Elisha returned just this spring. And now, in midsummer, everyone knew why he came back.

The women tested the stove before depositing their offerings and checked the fire as women did then and took their places with the others, sitting at the table or against the wall, separating themselves, as was the custom, from the men outside. They spoke in hushed tones, as people do at such times, and occasionally looked toward the doorway to the other part of the cabin, awaiting word of the battle going on there.

Only the sons were allowed in the death chamber of the dying lion; only they had permission from Mammy to sit or stand beside his deathbed. She would not have countenanced any loss of his dignity from those who would see only the tatters of his life in its final moments. This was her role and had been for years; not even Mary, the old man's last wife, had Mammy's power, and she was relegated to the kitchen with the daughters.

Mammy was the last autocrat of the family, the final arbiter of the memories of a forgotten age, and everyone deferred to her. She was the last living daughter of the old man's first wife, and the older sister of all his children, regardless of their dams. She had brought her family and all the families through the War and through the hard times that followed, and she had their respect and their awe. Some of the younger people at the deathwatch did not know her real name, which was Dorcas, the name Elisha gave her in honor of his mother, although he called her Belle when she was young, so many lifetimes ago. Even to her brothers she was Mammy, the matriarch, the one everyone turned to for counsel and comfort, the one everyone sought out in times of grief, for she had seen more than anyone and had become wise from it. And on this night, they had need of her again.

Beside the deathbed, young Will Hopkins struggled with his father. Elisha's sons, Hopkinses, Robinsons, or Blackburns, had taken turns holding the old man's wrists as he writhed in his delirium.

4

Starved for oxygen, his thin blood no longer able to feed his brain, the world around him, the world he would soon be leaving, had already been replaced. For days now, he had been speaking to the dead, and only Mammy knew his correspondents.

"Don't go, boys," the old man demanded, looking squarely into his son's eyes. "Don't go, I say!"

"Pappy, I ain't goin' nowhere," the confused young man said desperately, his voice cracking.

"Don't go, God damn it," he demanded. "Stay here."

He pulled again against his son's strong hands with amazing strength, and nearly slipped from his grasp.

"Please," he begged now. "Please stay with me."

"Mammy, what can I do?" the young man pleaded. "Why won't he listen to me?"

"Just hold on boy," she replied gently. "Don't let him go. Don't let him hurt himself." She knew he was almost gone. "It won't be long now."

She lit her pipe and walked over to the rocking chair where her black bonnet lay, the one she had worn for ten years now, the one she put on the day she buried Joseph, her second son, named for her Uncle Joseph, Elisha's brother. She had not taken it off in public since then. It was the same one she bought to wear to the older Joseph's grave, when she took his children to see where their father was buried, far into Kentucky where the hills could no longer be seen. It shaded her eyes when she went to the place where he lay, and no one could see her weep. She picked it up and placed it in her lap as she sat down. She took a long drag of the strong tobacco and finally spoke, the smoke curling from her mouth and nose:

"It ain't you he's talkin' to, son."

She was speaking to Will, Elisha's favorite, the son he named for the brother of the wife he loved the most, but she looked at his other sons as they watched their father's struggle. "It ain't you boys, either," she said as she looked around the tiny room.

There was George, her only full brother, and then the other boys, half-brothers all, but she loved them all, for they were all Elisha's sons. Why was it, she wondered, that although Elisha loved women so much, he cared so little for his daughters? Why was it that if he cared so much more for his sons he would defer to her alone? But even Mammy did not have the courage to ask such a question of him.

After a final spasm, the strength in the old man's arms failed and his head dropped back on the pillow. With the resistance gone from his father's arms, Will placed the great hands on his father's barely moving chest. The pleas from his lips were only whispers now, entreaties only a ghost could understand.

"Leave him be now," she said. "It weren't none of you boys he was callin' to."

With a sigh, she looked beyond the bed where the old man lay dying, beyond the lamplight that illuminated his shrunken frame, and through the tiny window at the full moon passing over the mountains. In the clouds that danced across it, she could see the shadows that haunted the old man and she knew they had come for him. She remembered them well: fiery young men who became warriors too soon, beautiful young girls who had not yet learned how much courage they would have to summon and how much loss they would have to endure. And of course the Indians, Elisha's most trusted friends, gone too. All of them gone; all ghosts, all of another age, of a time few in that cabin would have believed existed. And she spoke again, softly, as if she were in church, for she could feel his spirit departing:

"Bless their hearts," she said, a sad smile crossing her lips as she spoke. "Those boys went away a long time ago."

As the last breath passed from the old man's body and young Will fell sobbing against his father's now-lifeless form, she closed her eyes and spoke once more: "And they never come back."

Chapter One

Ariel in Twilight

"Look at that!" one of my fellow travelers said. "That's the Pacific Ocean!" It was our first view of the great western sea, and it was anticlimactic: we had not expected it to be an industrial blue-green, almost gray, reflecting the overcast sky. Perhaps we were subconsciously expecting palm trees and tropical lagoons even though we were on the cold and rainy North Pacific coast, far from Eastern Kentucky. But we were born and raised away from oceans, Atlantic or Pacific, and we weren't really sure what to expect.

We had burst though a gap in the mountains of the Coastal Range and were approaching Newport, Oregon. It was our destination for a week of training in dealing with disruptive students, the universal bane of modern school systems. We were all teachers or administrators, and behind our rental car were three carloads of teachers from other Eastern Kentucky counties. We had flown to Portland from Kentucky earlier that day and watched in wonder as we glided past regal Mount Hood before setting down at the airport.

"That's a hell of a mountain," said one of my companions, looking through the window of the airplane. "Look at the snow."

"It's a volcano," another, equally in awe, noted. "A real volcano."

After getting off the plane, we found our rental cars, loaded them, and headed out of Portland into the Willamette Valley, where fields stretched out in all directions, bursting with yellow winter wheat, as if it were the American Midwest. But nothing in the Midwest could compare to the giant white monolith that reminded us that we were far from the prairie and even farther from Kentucky. Throughout the drive, my companions would periodically turn around to watch Mt. Hood recede in the distance to reassure themselves that something that strange and majestic could really exist.

I had expected the Pacific Northwest to be different and it was. It was still spring in Kentucky and chilly the morning we flew out. The temperature in Oregon was much the same, although I was told that while the interior of the state would warm up rapidly, the coast would stay cool for most of the year. In Kentucky, we would soon be into summer, the hot and humid season, when the sun beats down on the mountains relentlessly, much as a slave overseer would oppress his charges before the Civil War.

Although uncomfortable, summer in Eastern Kentucky is at least more consistent than spring, the green and muddy season, when the earth softens and begins to ooze like an unhealed wound. Ruts form in the thin blacktop of mountain roads and the mud seeps through and covers everything on or beside the roads with a dull gray film, a last reminder of the cold days that had just passed. But spring it is a short season, and it fades into memory as lawn mowers sputter to life and begin their afternoon droning as men come home from work. Summer is long and productive, but fall is the best season, when the trees are clad in their autumn foliage and the days are warm and dry and the nights are crisp. For all its glory, fall in the mountains seems even shorter than spring, and the last season is always the hardest.

Winter closes in unexpectedly in Eastern Kentucky and the ground will freeze and heave up at night as the skies clear. The stars seem crystalline, almost touchable, like glass ornaments hanging from the limbs of Christmas trees. It is a time of penance and reflection, something required for the gift of the previous year's pleasures, an antidote to its excesses.

I could not imagine a place without seasons, but I was told there was little change on the Oregon coast, locked between the Coastal Range and the great thermal reservoir of the Pacific Ocean, but I did not think about it on this trip. Circadian rhythms were no more the reason I came to Oregon than to learn about how to discipline unruly students. For the entire week, my training was only the formal reason for my trip. There was a question nagging me and I hoped I could find the answer during the week.

It was cloudy on the coast, and we heard it rained up in Seattle about every other day, but we were farther south, not that far from California when we made Newport. We were all disappointed that the day was not brighter, but the first glimpse of the Pacific lifted our spirits when it came into view, even if it was not the deep blue of Hollywood movies.

We found our lodging, right on the beach, and began to settle in as the clouds suddenly dissipated and the sun poured through, warming us immediately. I looked for air-conditioning controls, but could find none. When I called the front desk, I was told that there were no controls because there was no air-conditioning in any of the rooms. The other people in my entourage were equally surprised at the lack of what is a stark necessity in the South, but since we had bright sunshine on only one or two days of the week that followed, we understood why cooling was unnecessary. Some of the rooms had fireplaces, however, and they were often used.

Indeed, we weren't in Kentucky anymore.

One day the sun came out especially bright after three days of chilly, heavily fogged mornings, and I was reminded of Kentucky during Indian summer. Something strange and magical happens then, after the winds have torn the last leaves from the trees and the hills have acquired their gray-brown coats for winter. For a few days, warmth and sunlight returns unexpectedly, and it is universally welcomed as birds sing, and insects, those not killed by the early frost, begin to buzz again.

The first settlers in America named it Indian summer, for it was the Indians who tried to tell them what was happening. At first they did not understand. They knew of brief respites in Old World winters; it was not unusual to have short periods of warm weather come after the first frost, and these abbreviated seasons were usually named for saints so that priests could claim another blessing for their church and offer another reason for fealty. There was All Hallows' summer or St. Luke's summer in England or l'été de la Saint-Martin in France and the resurgent warmth of those days supplied the analogy of Resurrection for the inevitable sermon that would follow.

But when the immigrants came to the New World, they found something much different. The Indians told them of it, and they could not believe it was more than what they had known in the old places, a few lukewarm days easily missed because of their brevity. But the Indians, having no reason to lie, spoke the truth. This season was nothing like what the settlers had known in the crowded cities they forsook and seemed to be part of a much older age of the earth, one that existed before priests and patriarchs came to usurp its message.

In the weary hills of Eastern Kentucky, in Pike County, the eastern arrowhead of the state of Kentucky, pushed between West Virginia and her maternal Virginia, Indian summer is stunning when it arrives. We are gifted with a holy season, an interlude of ghosts, and if we could remember what the Indians taught us, we would know this is the time when spirits are allowed to walk the earth again, when the earth is warmed one last time so it can be trod by weightless feet. This is the time when the dead are allowed to go in search of those they loved and those who loved them and, if the living will listen, offer their final good-byes or their last premonitions. But no one remembers the lesson anymore, just as few of us know that people lived in our hills a millennium before we arrived.

If Indian summer is especially brilliant, we can be deceived into thinking winter will not come at all, that the ice and snow will be deferred this time, that it will be warm and peaceful until spring. We will put on our summer clothes again and the girls will put on shorts to feel the sun on their legs, and those who have convertibles will drop the tops and ride into the warm breeze. And we will ignore the faint voices that seek us out, thinking them only the wind whistling through leafless trees. We will ignore the delicate tapping at the window or the odd zephyr rushing by us, and we will fail to look up at the stars at night, for we are busy and we are not our ancestors, who themselves forgot the lesson.

But for the past year, I had been relearning it as I had been relearning my family history, part of which led me to the western edge of America. I had a question I thought might be answered if I stood long enough on this rugged shoreline for it to come to me.

During the week that followed our settling in, we piled into our rental cars after class and explored the coastline, taking in the nearly deserted beaches and surreal rock outcroppings and watching kites soar in the relentless wind. One group drove all the way to the California state line just to say they had been there. We had only a week and crammed in all the sightseeing we could, drinking in the beauty and strangeness of the place.

The night before we went home, we had dinner at an Italian restaurant and shared our impressions of this alien place, or at least what we had seen of it, from the perspective of Eastern Kentuckians.

"Finally, some real American food," one of our party said. "I was gettin' tired of all that seafood."

"You don't like seafood?" I asked.

"Yeah, but not all the time," he replied. "My wife is crazy about snow crabs, though."

"Those Dungeness things are creepy," another said, referring to the huge crustaceans that were one of the prime culinary attractions of the area. "I've never seen anything that gross."

Our waitress, who had been listening surreptitiously to our conversation, raised her eyebrows.

"I don't think wine goes with something like that," he continued, looking at the two empty bottles of Oregon Merlot on our table. "I'd have to snap back a lot of Jack Black before I'd touch 'em."

"I wonder what the first settlers thought about them when they first came here," I ventured. "Must have been quite a change from Kentucky."

"Kentucky?" another one asked. "Kentuckians came out here?"

"Yeah," I replied. "Whole wagon trains of Eastern Kentuckians pulled out after the Civil War and went west. Some came here. Maybe not to the coast, but at least to Oregon."

"So why did they leave?" he asked.

"I guess to find work, like everyone else does," one of the women said. "To escape the poverty."

As I was growing up, I was not really aware that my family was poor or that all the families on Greasy Creek were poor, until "poverty" became the most common noun applied to Eastern Kentucky after President Johnson launched his War on Poverty there in the 1960's.

It had mixed results.

"We are poverty-stricken, you know" she said facetiously. "And if I don't start making some money, I'm going to quit teaching and get on the draw myself."

We laughed politely, but it was true that entire generations of Eastern Kentuckians had grown up on welfare since the president's visit. In some of our schools, over eighty percent of our students were on Medicaid. In our coal economy, jobs were scarce, but the worst part was that for some families there was no longer an impetus to find employment. After the last coal "boom" in 1973, the number of miners had dropped precipitously. With the mechanization that began in the 1950's and with the current preference for strip mining over deep mining, the coal industry had reduced its workforce to a fraction of the great hordes of men who once went into the pits. But with a generous public dole, some families had forgotten what it meant to be self-sustaining and that tragedy did not escape us, since as teachers we could see its effects every day.

"What about violence?" another asked. "Eastern Kentucky was supposedly pretty dangerous after the Civil War. Weren't most of the feuds caused by bad feelings from the War?"

"I thought the Hatfield-McCoy Feud was over a pig," someone replied.

"I thought it was over a woman," another commented.

"No, it had to be poverty," one of the women ventured. "If your family is starving, you'd fight for a pig or a chicken, wouldn't you?"

"I would," our waitress interjected.

"They have Civil War re-enactments here," I added.

"They fought the Civil War out here, too?" another asked.

"I don't think they actually had any Civil War battles out here," I said. "But there were a lot of Civil War veterans who came here after the War."

"I thought they just had whales," another opined.

One of the women pulled a brochure out of her purse and began reading: "Lincoln County extends for sixty miles up the central Oregon coast . . ." She read silently to herself and then said: "Yep, there it is. Civil War re-enactment at Fort Stephens."

"Well, this still ain't Myrtle Beach," another said. "I've been freezing my nuts off since I got here. I don't know why anyone would give up paradise to come to this place."

"Paradise? You mean, like, Pike County?" I teased.

"I'm from Floyd County, dude," he good-naturedly scowled. "Watch your mouth."

"I'm from Greasy Creek," I said, a little cocky from the wine we had already sampled. "That's paradise on earth."

"I'm from Mud Creek," he replied. "That's even better."

"Well, I'm ready for Paradise Regained," another teacher, obviously an English major, interjected. Our lips had been loosened somewhat, with the osso buco and the red wine that washed it down.

"Maybe paradise disappeared," I said. "Maybe they had to leave."

My companions looked at me questioningly.

"What do you mean?"

We ordered another bottle, and I offered to tell them about my research into my family history, which to my wonder, they readily accepted. I suppose I shouldn't have been surprised; most were baby-boomers like me, and were also beginning to look to their past. I was among the first of that storied group, but all of us were feeling our mortality, just as that entire American generation was crossing the half-century mark.

I told them about the project that was consuming me, a project that had begun the previous year, in the spring after my father's death, when the news of a major road reconstruction project was announced in Pike County. U.S. 460, one of the four major highways serving Pike County, was going to be rebuilt along a new path, ignoring the old roadway altogether. Part of that road would take my grandfather's home, the hollow where I grew up, and most importantly, my family cemetery. It was known as the Old Prater Cemetery, named for my mother's family, which had acquired the property from my father's family after the Civil War. Until I began my research, I did not know it was first a Hopkins family cemetery, although every year I tended the graves of Hopkinses and Praters, just as my father did, and my grandfather before him.

It had fallen to me to identify the unknown graves on the Old Prater before construction began and I plunged into the past to try to find who was buried in the dozens of graves that were never decorated and had no formal markers. It became an obsession, and I battled the Kentucky Department of Transportation for nearly six years to give me some assistance, but it was basically up to me to determine if those graves would have stones with something other than "Unknown" engraved on them.

I was not that successful, but what I learned was worth the effort. I learned that my family had lived for the better part of two centuries around that sacred spot, along with an even older, nearly destroyed Hopkins cemetery below the Old Prater. But what I also found in my research was that there had been another life in the hills of Eastern Kentucky long before the coal industry came. There had been real people who lived their lives in relative peace, raised their families with no concept of danger, and went to their graves with the satisfaction of knowing they had accomplished much in the time they had, until the Civil War came and destroyed nearly everything they had built, and more importantly, nearly everything they believed.

Such occurrences were not uncommon to my dinner group, and we began to share similar experiences. We had much the same history in Pike as in Floyd County and I eagerly probed their memories. I was looking for information wherever I could find it.

I could speak very authoritatively about Eastern Kentucky and about the War, since I had done my research and I was publishing a book on my family. I felt a little guilty about impressing my colleagues, however, since what I did not tell them was that I had only recently learned my family history, and only by necessity. Actually, I had relearned it and not all of it, for I had been told stories about my people many years before and had dismissed them as mere fairy tales told to me by my grandmother. Now I knew differently, and on the last night of my visit to Oregon, I was looking for the answer to a question that had arisen during my research, a question I could not answer in Eastern Kentucky.

We consumed another bottle of wine before we left the restaurant, and after we paid the bills, we got into our cars and drove carefully back to our motel. No one wanted to exceed the speed limit and risk a DUI in a strange state, especially one where the jail menu might include Dungeness crabs.

Still a little tipsy from the evening, I changed into a sweat suit when I returned to my room and walked down to the beach to clear my head and watch the moonlight on the water. I thought of the beloved grandmother who told me the family stories and I wished she could have seen this place. She had been dead for twenty years, but I had been thinking of her almost continually since the death of my father, but his death wasn't the only reason for my thoughts of her. My grandmother was the only one who could have told me who was buried in all those nondescript mounds of earth on the Old Prater Cemetery, and the responsibility of learning who they were weighed heavily on me. Even after writing my book, I still had unanswered questions about my past.

In my research I learned that some of my family had indeed gone to distant places, and Oregon was one of them, where land was cheap or free. Although I knew their descendants were somewhere nearby, I did not look for them nor expect to find them on this trip. I was there for a different reason: I had a question and only a ghost could have truly answered it.

It is easy to believe in ghosts; if you believe in angels, then the extrapolation follows. Indeed, I sometimes feel I was told those stories about my family by a messenger seraph, effectively disguised as my grandmother, a purposeful angel who had given up her wings for a sojourn on earth. At the time she told me her tales, I attached nothing special to them, although there were times that even as a child I knew there was something transcendental about her words, especially when she spoke of people that neither I nor she had ever known.

Occasionally, a winter storm would cut the power to Greasy Creek and my grandmother would take down one of the kerosene lamps she always kept on the mantle for just such emergencies. At such times, I knew a story about the Old Ones, as she called them, would be forthcoming. The Old Ones were the pioneers, those who settled Greasy Creek, those who paid in toil and sweat for the land I grew up on, those who had never seen an electric light, although I had begun my own life without the benefit of one. Electricity did not come to Greasy Creek until 1949, three years after I was born, and it was still unreliable as I was growing up. Nearly everyone kept kerosene lamps and used them regularly, and I often looked forward to the lights going out when I stayed with her because I knew a special tale would soon follow.

There would be a subtle shift in the way she told her stories at those times, as if her grandson was not the only one listening. It was as if someone else was in the dimly lit room, making sure the tale was told properly, and I could almost feel that presence. I know now that at such times, I was privy to secrets that no other family had, and I still mourn for their loss.

My grandmother's name was Rissie Hopkins Damron Prater, and she was a younger sister of Frank Hopkins, my real grandfather, who had given her his gravely ill, last child. Frank had lost his first wife and his first son in one of the waves of influenza attacks that plagued the coalfields of Eastern Kentucky constantly after the First World War. His second son, Marvin, the child who would grow up to become my father, was near death, dysenteric and feverish, and my grandfather, shattered by the loss of his wife and first son, could not handle another funeral. Rissie, born with a cleft palate and a clubfoot and subject to the cruelties untutored children inflict on each other, was nineteen and unmarried. She did not expect ever to marry and she had taken Marvin because she loved him and vowed that he would not die in spite of all the odds against him. Indeed, he survived, and all of Greasy Creek was amazed that she had won such a battle. When my grandfather finally put his life together again, and came to take back his son, Rissie would not give him up.

"He's mine, Frank," she said. "You gave him to me and you can't have him back for all time." My grandfather had never seen such fire, or such love, in her eyes and knew he had no choice but to accept the shared custody she offered him. And when she married, she demanded that her new husband accept Marvin as their son. And he did so willingly, for by then he loved Marvin as much as he loved Rissie. His name was Harlen Damron, the handsomest man on Greasy Creek, the man Rissie had loved at a distance for her whole life, and the man she thought she could never have. But she did not know until he proposed that he had loved her across the same divide.

Harlen died in 1940, mortally wounded by a roof fall in the old Greasy Creek mine as it was being junked for the steel tracks that would be melted down to go into the armaments that would soon be needed in World War II. When we took up his grave as the cemetery was being moved, there was little left of the body that had been placed there over sixty years before, but the skull was a source of wonder to the gravediggers and me. Although most of his bones had returned to the earth, his skull would have been the perfect laboratory specimen, with its perfect teeth, except where two had been knocked out in the trauma of the roof fall, and a slightly misaligned occipital plate to reveal the wound that took his life.

Jesus, I thought as I held his skull in my hands, she said he was so perfect, and I thought she was just remembering fondly the man she loved. " Look at this," I said to the gravediggers. "There isn't a cavity or a filling in any of his teeth."

It was more proof of the veracity of my grandmother's stories.

She said the undertaker told her he had never seen such a physical specimen as Harlen in all his days. I had seen only pictures of him, including the startlingly clear glass portrait of him locked into the marble tombstone she had purchased for his grave. I was born six years after he died, the same amount of time I eventually spent on the cemetery where he was buried, pondering my task, sitting beside his grave and wondering who were the people buried near him in graves marked only by fieldstones or not marked at all, and wishing that I could remember everything she said, everything she told me about my people.

I remember well the story of his last hours in the hospital room, with pneumonia raging through his body and how he willed himself to press back the delirium to make his last testament to her. I could easily see the family lined up outside his room; I could smell the iodoform on the dressing of his wound and I could hear his last whispers as he looked at the only woman he ever loved for the last time. I grew up as close to him as my father would have wanted because of Rissie's stories, and when I saw his bones and his nearly perfect skull, I knew her stories were true and I was ashamed that I had doubted her.

In the green nursery of my youth, I did not realize that all her stories were true, and not mere entertainment for a restless child and that telling them was something sacred to her. I have since learned why she told them to me and I expect I will go to my grave still furious at myself for not paying more attention. At odd times, something that she told me thirty, forty, or even fifty years ago will suddenly come back and I will frantically write it down for fear that it will not come again. During classes that week in Oregon, I often made notes as boredom nudged out my conscious state and allowed me a fleeting glimpse of some scene she had described almost a half-century before.

Writing down such thoughts is a tenet of what I tried to teach my students over thirty years of grading essays, and I am finally practicing what I preached. I am haunted now by too many missed opportunities and too many gentle ghosts who require me to fulfill the promise Rissie made to them and left the debt to me.

My grandmother was like a West African griot relaying the history of a village and she told the stories with the reverence demanded of such an awesome task. Every time I discovered something new in my search for my family, I would have a tingle of déjà vu from something she had told me decades before. Perhaps I may be forgiven that lack of concentration since I did not then appreciate the matrix of her stories. I did not know that most of the hard times she spoke of were caused by the great American Civil War, and that the sheltered hills of Eastern Kentucky were no more removed from the holocaust of that war than the cornfields of Virginia or the rolling plains of Tennessee. I did not know that the fierce battles she spoke of actually happened and that the people who fought them had my blood running through their veins and that they lived and breathed and labored and sweated and loved. And most of all, I did not know that she was passing on a sacred duty to me, one she probably thought she had failed to impart, one that I did not obey until it was nearly too late to make a difference.

And who had passed them on to her? The oldest stories were those told to her by her own grandmother, Dorcus Hopkins Lewis, the daughter of Elisha Hopkins, one of the most legendary characters of Greasy Creek. Rissie called her Mammy, as did everyone else, whether or not they were of her blood. Mammy was a black-bonneted mountain Ariel, as fiercely protective of the family stories as she was of the family itself. And like Ariel, the Hebrew lioness of God she emulated, she would not have the stories altered. They had to be told properly, to an audience that would appreciate their worth.

I suspect that is why I knew that those stories were different from the ones Rissie told me about the people I remembered. She told me of my grandfather Frank and his brother Bud and the boys of Greasy Creek going off to the Great War. She told me about their return to the horror of the great Spanish influenza epidemic, where Frank lost his mother, his first wife, my real grandmother, and his first son in that great national tragedy. She still wept when she told me how he nearly went mad because of it.

She spoke painfully of the Depression and the war that followed it. She told me where she was when she heard the news of Pearl Harbor, and how my father had to go off to fight the same people my grandfather did a generation before. And she told me of other boys of Greasy Creek, those who returned and those who did not. She told me accurately of the countless losses in war and in the Greasy Creek mine, for indeed coal mining was a form of war; a war against the mountain that grudgingly gave up its riches, although no coal miner ever grew wealthy in the pits and the mountain extracted a harsh price from the miners for its injury.

But her words changed when she talked about the Old Ones, the people who settled Greasy Creek and wrested a life from hills still covered with thousand-year-old trees. Even she could not have remembered what it was like then, for the trees themselves fell a decade before she was born. And that loss came even more decades after a greater tragedy, after the War had taken nearly everything that was beautiful in that life and replaced it with something no one could have prepared for. Somehow, I knew it was not really her speaking when she told me of those days.

When she spoke of the Old Ones, it was Mammy's words she used and somewhere in the darkness of the room where I listened, fending off sleep, there was Mammy's spirit, listening to Rissie as I was listening, making sure that her granddaughter told her stories correctly.

I would sometimes be confused when she spoke of those people because I did not know them, and could not comprehend old people doing the things young people would be doing, like riding horses, and having dances, or courting each other. I could not understand how old people would be able to climb on a horse with their canes and trembling hands and shuffling gait. And dance? The old people I knew in my youth seemed always to be in fear of falling and breaking a hip. Some ancient friend of my grandmother was always bedfast, and the smell of urine, no matter how faint, would accentuate our visits to their sickrooms, and it did not seem long afterward that a funeral would be preached. How could they ever have danced, I wondered? And why would old people be interested in courting other old people?

I couldn't imagine the attraction of weathered, wrinkled old bodies to other equally desiccated forms. But I was merely a child, of course, and could not fathom the concept that old people could once have been young. Nor did I consider the possibility that people, if they live long enough, grow old, or that I would grow old myself. In my child's view of the world, nothing ever changed.

I suspect these things contributed to my blithe dismissal of my grandmother's stories as fantasy; I never asked her about the Old Ones after I grew up. I could not comprehend a life that did not include the culture of coal mining, and for all the intellectual growth I should have gleaned from my college life, I was still prejudiced toward my past. How could I relate to a world where young men did not become old men too soon, where the creases around their eyes and cheeks were not indelibly marked with coal dust, as if they had webs of black tattooed into their skin?

But it was not merely the trappings of the world she tried to impart to me; it was something else, something more intangible. It was the sense of that world and that was what Mammy had given to her. It was grand and glorious and although she never spoke of castles and kings and beautiful princesses, I was sure they existed. Their days were always bright and the nights were eternally starlit and the air was so pure it would be painful to breathe. Unicorns pawed impatiently on the hillside, demanding that someone play with them, and butterflies swarmed by the millions.

But I felt that way only as a child.

When I grew up, I concluded that nothing so awesome and grand could have ever flourished on Greasy Creek, whose center was the decaying remnant of an old coal town. Eventually, I lost the wonder I once had in my grandmother's stories, but I never lost the apprehension, for there were other things in her tales: twisted, sinister things. She did not have to speak of them, but I knew they lurked somewhere about. Unlike a mere teller of fairy tales, she would never let me think that goodness could live forever, and if goodness departs, what replaces it? She could never bring herself to suggest to me that, in spite of my childish expectations, worlds do not ultimately end. Until I grew older, I would ask her: "Did they live happily ever after?"

"For a while," she would say. "For a little while."

If I assigned moats and castles to their lives it was not her fault. She did not tell me the men were gallant knights in armor; I made that up myself. She did not tell me there were Guineverean revelries in May; I added the stage dressings myself. She did not tell me of bright swords and wizards; I created them in my own imagination.

Neither did she tell me of dragons, but I knew they were there, and even after I had given up believing in them, the unease remained. And now I know they were there, and the terrible fire they exhaled consumed everything, leaving only a sulfurous aura that a century-and-a-half of fierce spring rains has yet to fully erase. Twenty years after she spoke her last word to me, I began to learn why she never told me of them before. And on the last night of my visit to Oregon, I still had not found the answer to my question.

The wind had calmed and the moon was descending, slipping in and out of the clouds, and barely illuminating the wet strand before me. Unlike the crowded southern beaches I had visited, Oregon's coast is largely empty and remarkably pristine. It is a little wild and somewhat primordial, as if one almost expects dinosaurs to be still be lurking in the headlands, especially at night with the crashing surf drowning out everything but thought.

About a mile down the beach, I saw a huge bonfire with a few people attending it. Wondering who would have a bonfire so late, I jogged down to talk to three men who were watching it. They were all dressed in work clothes, and an idling John Deere skidder with logging tines sat not far away. I was not unfamiliar with the machine; I had sold them at a heavy equipment dealership where I worked during a time when I was not teaching.

"Where are the marshmallows?" I asked as I approached them.

"Fresh out!" one of them smiled. "You missed your chance."

"You all do this often?" I asked, the wine having made me a little more gregarious than usual.

"All the damn time," one of them replied. "After storms, we get a shitload of debris on the beach. We pile it up, dry it out, and torch it."

I readily understood what he said about storms. Earlier that week a squall had blown up after midnight and awakened me with the rain beating a machine-gun rhythm on the door to my motel room and soaking the carpet in front of the door. When the lightning flashed, I could see the surf violently pounding the shoreline. The next morning, the beach was littered with driftwood.

"That explains some of the ash piles I've seen," I said. "I just thought y'all just threw a lot of beach parties around here."

"Well, that too," he grinned. "But some of these old logs have been in the water for a hundred years." He pointed to a great rotted specimen decorated with seaweed not far from the tractor. "That one is still pretty soggy. It'll be summer before we can burn it."

I looked at the crumbling but nearly intact log as he issued a warning: "You don't want to walk on the beach during a storm. These damned things will fly out of the surf on you."

I wondered if my people could have cut that tree. Wouldn't that be ironic, I thought, to be killed by a tree someone of my blood chopped down a century ago? It would make for an interesting headline in the Pike County paper: "Local Man Killed By Tree Thought To Have Been Cut By Relatives A Hundred Years Ago."

I chatted with the workers a while longer and decided to walk on up the beach for a mile or two before I turned back to the Newport lights. My eyesight adjusted to the darkness after being seduced by the bonfire's flames and I began to see clearly again. The moon was down and the sky had cleared. I had never seen so many stars before. I knew I would have to come here again, and bring with me the family I still had. I wanted my wife to see this wild shoreline with me, this place that rarely knew hurricanes like the southern beaches we both loved, but which was constantly buffeted by storms and rain.

This is the essential difference between the two coasts, I thought. Life is illusory in the South, too gentle and too protected, until the hurricanes come. Unlike the denizens of this place, we are lulled into too much complacency, and we are not always prepared for danger. Out here, nature reminds one constantly of its power.

As I walked down that deserted beach I again felt sharply the loss of my father and I wished that I could have brought him out here before he died. At least he had seen the ocean as he boarded a troop ship for Europe, but I wanted him with me on that beach. I wanted family to be with me, sharing this experience, but my father was gone, my mother would never make such a trip at her age, and my grandmother had long passed beyond the pale. I wished I could have told her of my trip, but she was over two decades in her grave. She told me once that she would like to have seen the ocean, but it didn't matter, as long as her children had the chance. That was typical of Rissie.

I wondered if the others in my unsteady dinner party had a grandmother like mine, or if they felt the same way I did about our past. I suspect they did, on both counts; as facetious as our comments were about the paradise of Eastern Kentucky, there was no denying the strange and powerful attachment we had for home. The émigrés of long ago had it too, and a hundred years ago, there were no coal mines to shut down and force our people to leave home to find work as I did. Yet something compelled them to go far away with no plans to ever return.

Rissie told me stories of Greasy Creek's young men going off to fight in strange lands and how those who returned, including my father, came home to a place little changed from what they remembered and how they swore they would never leave again. They had seen the world and could live without it. But in her other stories, Mammy's stories, she told me of boys who did not go to the other side of the world to fight alien people. They fought at home, against young men with whom they had grown up. They tried to kill the same boys who had hunted with them, fished with them, swam with them, and shared their boyhood dreams. And when they came home, the world they left was gone.

Mammy's stories were confirmed and supplemented by my research, and the things I found in footnotes of the most obscure history texts amazed me. I learned that a former vice president of the United States, the Southern candidate for president before the Civil War, fled to Pike County after a futile attempt to prevent the War. John Cabell Breckinridge knew he had friends there who would protect him from the federal troops who sought to arrest him for treason. After three days among his friends, part of the time drinking my great-great-great-grandfather's whiskey, he went on to Virginia to tell Jefferson Davis that he had decided to cast his lot with the Confederacy.

Rissie told me how Mammy had loved a "great man" with blue eyes; that she had loved him from a distance, and that she had last seen him when he spent the night at her father's farm. Until I came upon the facts, I would not have believed she was speaking of the same man. Our family was just another clan of Eastern Kentucky coal miners, I thought, and we would never have had a brush with one of the most important men of the Southern cause.

Yet the story was true.

I also learned that James Garfield, a future president of the United States, had been made a brigadier general in the Union Army in Pikeville, the county seat of Pike County, after his greatest victory, only to have Abraham Lincoln himself ask him a year later to resign his commission and return to politics in Ohio where the president needed him more. The great Northern newspapers ran stories on his success, perhaps to counterbalance the spate of bad news for the Union as the War began, although the history books now say little about Garfield's time in the mountains.

Before he won the presidency, Garfield revisited Pike County and spoke fondly of his work here, but he was assassinated soon after taking the nation's highest office. Only a weathered highway marker in the Pikeville city park makes note of it, and one has to wonder how well now-devastated Eastern Kentucky would have fared had he lived longer. Would he have allowed the place where his march to the White House began to have suffered what it did after the War? Would he have allowed the speculators to buy up the timber and mineral rights of the mountaineers on the cheap and then ruthlessly exploit them for a hundred years afterward? Would he have allowed the sinister legacy of the War to haunt us through today?

I discovered what the War did to my homeland through my research, but I somehow knew it before I opened the first dusty file in the Kentucky State Archives. I learned that Union guns had shelled Pikeville to force out the occupying Confederates and that the town changed hands seven times during the conflict. No teacher had told me this when I was growing up; no books told me of what my people endured and I was perplexed as to why all of this had been hidden from me, from all of us in Pike County. It seemed almost that there had been a conspiracy to deny us our heritage.

I read of a great army that had marched through the county in 1864 on its way to Saltville, Virginia to destroy the saltworks there and deprive the South of its last vital staple and starve it into submission. The battle received little note in the history books, perhaps because the battle was one of the last Confederate victories before loss of the War itself. The Battle of Saltville was eclipsed by the surrender at Appomattox six months later, but it was fought largely between Kentuckians, mostly Eastern Kentuckians, many with kinsmen on the opposite side. Yet Kentucky history books almost universally fail to mention it.

And more personally, I learned that same army marched back from its defeat with prisoners from my family, and led one to his doom and caused another, when all was lost, to become one of the last protectors of the very symbol of the Confederacy, President Jefferson Davis himself. In my youth, I did not know the story she told me of those last days were true, but with everything I learned in my research, I finally began to understand my grandmother's stories, or at least understand why she told them to me, long after I had forgotten most of them.

I knew that, I would think when I came across another confirmation of Rissie's stories, when the electric sensation crawled up from the base of my spine. I knew that already!

They were Rissie's stories, but it was Mammy's shade, still clad in her black bonnet, smoking her corncob pipe, making sure that I got the story right and that I would retell the stories properly someday, for they are not mine to tell. If they were, I would have given them happy-ever-afters. I would portray the Civil War as merely an interlude in the lives of the boys of Greasy Creek, who would come home to raise their children with the girls they left behind them. I would have those children grow up and present their parents with grandchildren, and in the fading light of their last years, I would have them come to play at the feet of their forebears. And I would have those boys grow old and bask in the honor of service to the countries that claimed their hearts when they were young, when they were not crippled and arthritic and could ride for days on little food and sleep. I would have them brag to their grandchildren of the heroic deeds they once performed. And I would reluctantly consign them to the grave after wondrous, long lives of increase and accomplishment.

But that would not be true, for it did not happen that way for my family, or for any of so many other families on Greasy Creek or in any of the peaceful glades and quiet coves and green hollows of Eastern Kentucky. The War and its aftermath was a stark time, a time of unrelenting pain, and it buffeted my people with a force no less destructive than the eruption of Mount Hood's sister ravaged this western state a century later, and it lasted for decades after the last musket was fired.

I am not the least surprised now that some of my family sought refuge from the tragedy on the featureless plains of Minnesota or Nebraska or that some made the long trek all the way to the place I now stood.

That was the real reason for my trip to Oregon: I wanted to see, if I could, what my people saw when they came here. I wanted to see if living in the shadow of mountains that still smoked after a million years would have been adequate compensation for abandoning the worn hills that sheltered them in Eastern Kentucky. I wanted to see if the thick forests and rich valleys of the Northwest would have given them the living they could not have made amid the tumult of Pike County after the Civil War. But I wanted most to see if their spirits would come to me somehow and tell me that their new lives made it all worthwhile.

But none came.

There were no visions on that rugged shore the last night I was there and I left with my question unanswered. Perhaps my grandmother had already told me the answer long ago and I had forgotten it. Perhaps my great-great-grandmother would no longer channel messages to me because of my callowness.

Or perhaps there was no answer for spirits to give.

I believe now, after I have seen how my people went nearly as far from Kentucky as men and women could have gone in those days, and after they unloaded their wagons to begin the very last chapter of their lives, that they would not have been able to answer the one simple question I wanted to ask them:

Were you ever sure, even in this distant, lonely place, that you were far enough from home to find peace?

Chapter Two

Birds

Lyndon Baines Johnson, the thirty-sixth president of the United States, came to Pike County on a cold day in October of 1968, almost as a fugitive. Pike County was a stop on the campaign trail for Hubert Humphrey, since Johnson had recently declared that he would neither seek nor accept his party's nomination for another term. He came to that conclusion after realizing that the country would never re-elect him because of the war in Vietnam.

The formal reason for the president's visit was to dedicate the new Fishtrap Dam on the Levisa Fork of the Big Sandy River, just above where it joins the Russell Fork near Greasy Creek. The dam had been built to save downstream towns from the nearly annual flooding that had ravaged them, and had been built with federal money since the state had none to spend on us. Four years earlier, Johnson had come to Eastern Kentucky to declare his War on Poverty, and Appalachia was its major theater. It struck me that since the war in Vietnam had already cost him his political career and was appearing increasingly unwinnable, Johnson must have wanted to end public life with at least one clear victory in some kind of war.

I was in my last year at Pikeville College and working part-time in television news, so I had a ringside seat to the ceremonies. Here was the president himself and various luminaries visiting our snake-bitten county, where over half the homes had no inside bathrooms and were usually heated with coal in either open grates or Warm Morning stoves. Overnight snowfalls would be covered with a fine layer of gray ash by noontime and the omnipresent smell of sulfur was a constant reminder of our subservience to the mineral, but there were few jobs available in the coal industry in 1968. Most of the year's high school graduates had already gone north to find work.

Regardless of why he was here, the president's visit, within a few miles of my home, was a historic moment for me and I could not wait to tell my grandmother about it. I owed her a story or two, considering how many she had told me when I was growing up, although at twenty-two I had already begun to forget most of them.

Johnson spoke of how the dam would tame the river, and how Pikeville and the rest of the towns below the dam would flourish without the constant threat the river offered them. There would be no more flooding in the Big Sandy Valley, he told us, and a new prosperity would come back to the hills. A pair of raucous crows in the treetops seemed to take issue with the president's speech and flew noisily away when he went on to harangue the crowd to vote for Humphrey in the coming presidential election. If we voted for "that skunk" Richard Nixon, he said, projects like these would never be seen again.

Humphrey did not win, but that did not stem the flow of antipoverty money into the hills. Succeeding Democratic or Republican administrations recognized the political advantage of doling out money to get Pike County votes, but the boon of the dam was not as great as was promised. Runoff from strip mines continued to flow into the Big Sandy and the pool behind the lake on the Levisa filled with layers of silt, diminishing its capacity to hold water, and the valley still floods, although the dam does an excellent job of collecting garbage flung into it upstream.

Maybe the crows knew something we didn't.

As I listened to the president's speech, I wondered if there was ever a time when Pike County was prosperous, when its residents were self-supporting and did not have to leave home to find work. I was lucky in that my father had a good job in the mines and was now politically connected enough to secure me a teaching job when I graduated from college, but I had been part of the high school exodus in 1964 and I had returned from Ohio only the previous year. Most of my class stayed up north and I would not see many of them again until they retired, when they came back to the hills to live out the life that was denied them when we were young.

And in all the speeches that wintry day, the river was portrayed as a monster, a villain, something that destroyed our society instead of helping it, and I casually wondered then if there was ever a time the river was benevolent. Only after several more presidents did I learn that once upon a time the river was indeed a friend.

By the time of the Civil War, Pike County was a genuine river culture, as was every county that lined the banks of the Big Sandy as it desultorily flowed toward the Ohio. Steamboats would begin regular service by November and end at Easter, although traffic could continue all summer in a wet year. On the river, the farthest reaches of Kentucky's eastern border were easily accessible, and Pikeville, the county seat, was a somewhat cosmopolitan village for its time. Merchants came from Indiana and Ohio to establish businesses and profited from sending and receiving cargoes. Little thought was given to overland shipping, except for cattle.

There were only two true roads in the county, both poorly maintained and both leading to Virginia: the Mount Sterling-Pound Gap Road went south to cross the border ridge of Pine Mountain, and the Old Virginia Turnpike followed the Levisa Fork east and skirted the mountain ridge. In Virginia, it was known as the Old Kentucky Turnpike, but its nomenclature in either state belied its primitive condition.

In 1860, Pike County was linked less to Kentucky than it was to Virginia, which surrounded it on two of three sides, and in fall the roads saw vast herds of cattle and hogs surging from oak grove to oak grove toward the mother state, dining on the mast of acorns under them. Although many of the mountain men did not know it, those journeys to eastern markets were preparing them for the great cattle drives of the western plains by men forced out of the hills by the Civil War and the violence that followed it. For the rest of the century, in Texas and Kansas and other states across the Mississippi, many Eastern Kentuckians worked famously the trade they perfected here.

The Mount Sterling-Pound Gap road was planned to be a way to divert that trade as well as the steamboat trade from the Big Sandy and the great cities of Cincinnati and Louisville on the Ohio to the Bluegrass and Lexington, which still has a rivalry with its larger siblings. Lexington was near the Kentucky River, which rises across the mountains in neighboring Letcher County, but steamboats could not ply the upper reaches of the Kentucky, whereas the Big Sandy could boast regular traffic to Pikeville since 1837. When water levels permitted, boats steamed even further upstream to the mouth of Greasy Creek, where the Levisa Fork that Johnson dammed and the Russell Fork combine to form a navigable stream and goods flowed both ways. Resultantly, the denizens of the Big Sandy generally ignored the Bluegrass town.

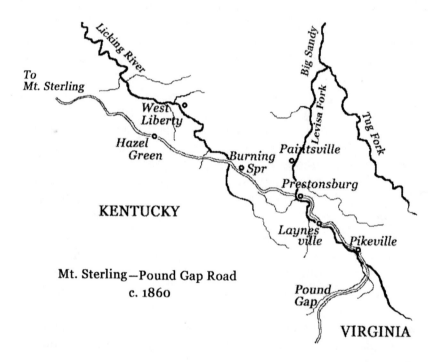

Mt. Sterling—Pound Gap Road
c. 1860

One of the products they shipped downriver was hemp, which was used to make rope and burlap for the cotton bales that were streaming out of New Orleans by the millions every year. They needed hemp and Pike County had plenty of it, growing wild here and flourishing on the hillsides and boggy creek banks. The first Indians who lived here made mats from it for their homes, as did the Cherokee when they arrived later. White families learned to use it when they came, but more often simply packed down the dirt floors of their cabins, and sold the hemp down the river.

When the mines came after 1900, hemp growing expanded with nonnative varieties introduced as well. Rope was constantly in demand in the mining operations, and hardworking farmers always had a market, but profit was low. Eventually hemp farming was abandoned as men gave up toiling in the fields for the steady paychecks they got from the mines. The hillsides grew up again, and no one thought to eradicate the aromatic plants that came back year after year. For decades hemp grew without cultivation in the hollows of Pike County. It was as common as the butterflies that came back every spring.

But the miners' paychecks appeared only as long as the men were able to work or the mines stayed open, so families kept their gardens and chicken coops and hogpens. They also kept their milk cows, and hemp became more than a nuisance; it was dangerous. My uncle Avery Prater used to pay me to pull up the plants that grew wild in Snake Branch, where my family had lived for over a century, because "it would make the cows' milk taste funny." There was so much of it that in fall the pungent aroma of ripe marijuana would fill the hollows and I never knew what it was that I was pulling up until I got to college. In the 1950's I probably destroyed what would today be a million dollars' worth of quite marketable pot.

One evening my Aunt Ola, Avery's wife, called the house to ask me to come up and bring in the cattle since it was long past milking time and they had not appeared. It was the early 1960's, and I had been too busy with schoolwork to make my annual hemp assault. When she called, I left immediately, fearing the cows had gotten sick from eating too much of the evil weed. I followed the usual trail up the mountain, guided by the occasional tinkle of the cowbells, until I found the three missing bovines calmly chewing their cud with distended udders ready for milking, but they paid no attention to me as I approached them.

That's strange, I thought. They usually move when they see me coming.

I made a display of cutting a large switch to threaten them, which always had an immediate effect, but they ignored me. Although I hated striking an animal, I whacked each of their bony rumps, but they kept chewing. I tried to pull them with their bell straps, but they would not move. I even tried pushing them off the hill, but they merely farted and refused to look in my direction.

For a moment I thought I detected a shared grin among them.

I was flabbergasted; I had never seen them behave like that. What I didn't know was that the cows were happily regurgitating the plants from their stomachs to chew their cud and neither they nor I knew that process was squeezing out every last molecule of THC in the hemp plants they had eaten.

They were stoned, of course.

Eventually, I admitted defeat and walked off the mountain to tell my aunt that I had failed. It was long past dark when I got back to her house without them and apologized for my lack of success.

"I'm sorry, Aunt Ola," I said. "I don't know what's the matter. They wouldn't move."

"Don't worry about it," she said with a sigh. "They'll come in when they're ready." Apparently, she had seen them that way before.

In college, I saw that same phenomenon all over again on several occasions. "Damn, man," some of my friends would say. "I am wrecked." There was the same bovine expression in their faces that I saw in those cows, and I finally understood my uncle's rationale.

Hemp growing was almost forgotten when plans were announced to rebuild U.S. 460, which generally followed the route of the Old Virginia Turnpike, and the Kentucky Department of Transportation upset more than a few people who had hoped the new road would take their property and give them the means to leave for better climes. The new right-of-way, the KYDOT said, would largely ignore the old road in order to minimize disruption of businesses and homes that lined the road almost all the way to the Virginia line. The cost of displacing these people would have been far more than the cost of blasting through the mountains instead of going around them. It was a new concept and would cause much less inconvenience to far fewer people, the KYDOT noted, as the road would be much straighter.

But inconvenience is a relative term, since the new roadway took my family cemeteries and Snake Branch, where the cows got stoned, and where my ancestral home had stood for a hundred years, and it was inconvenient to me. And the new plans were not as modern as the KYDOT thought they were, since animals had traversed those hills, stamping down permanent ruts for centuries, before the white men or the Indians came here. The KYDOT was just learning the concept of taking the path of least resistance, although the buffalo had learned it ages before, probably from their dinosaur ancestors.

As a boy, I stumbled over those paths many times, the same paths followed by hoofed creatures for eons. My father had used them as well, as did my grandfather and all the people of my family going back to the first Hopkins in Pike County, my great-great-great-great grandfather Cornelius, who came here in 1822 with a land grant for fifty acres on the waters of the Big Sandy River.

Cornelius and his wife Dorcus Thacker Hopkins lived at the mouth of Greasy Creek until the Civil War came and Elisha, his first son and my great-great-great grandfather, moved his parents deep into Greasy Creek and built a cabin for them where they would be safe. It was on a knoll overlooking the forks of Greasy Creek, and when they died they were buried there, above the old Hopkins burying ground. What eventually became the Old Prater Cemetery, named for another of my ancestors, was created with Cornelius's death.

He was in his eighties during the War; too old to fight off the depredations of the roving gangs that preyed on everyone, regardless of their political sympathies. Cornelius did not want to leave the land that he had carved from the wilderness with his own hands, but he had to trust his son.

By 1860, Elisha had built a life for himself and his three families and was in business with his brother Joseph, who was quite content with only one family. The issue of wives was the only material thing the two brothers disagreed on. Joseph felt that his success required a certain observance of the rules of society, since Pike County had been in existence only since 1821, he had to do his part to help civilization take root, not to mention the fact that his wife relished her role as part of that emerging society. With Joseph's success, she demanded that he build her a new house of cut lumber instead of one of the log cabins that most Pike Countians used for homes. It was not as warm as a cabin was, and it creaked when the wind blew, but it was painted a bright yellow that stood out brightly, and most of the other wives on Shelby Creek envied her. She also boasted a real iron cooking stove in the kitchen, while many families cooked on open hearths.

Elisha Hopkins could not have cared less about the trappings of civilization; he had seen his father destitute from losing nearly everything they had in Virginia and he wanted no truck with a society that elevated bankers and judges to positions of prominence. He built sturdy cabins for his three families and owed no man anything when he finished them. He hated banks with a passion and had good reason. In the Panic of 1819, bankers all along the East Coast began calling in notes and demanding hard federal currency in payment. They would not accept the paper notes they themselves had issued and neither would they exchange their own paper money for federal dollars. Many farmers simply went broke and pulled up stakes for the West, which usually meant Kentucky. Cornelius lost nearly everything he had, but managed to hold on to seventy-two acres, although he knew he could not continue paying the high taxes Virginia was assessing. So he acquired a land grant and went alone to Kentucky, to where many of his wife's family had already migrated, to start a new life.

In 1824, after two years of backbreaking work with only one visit back to see his family, Cornelius was ready to move them to their new home. He waited until autumn and sold or stored his crops and returned to sell his seventy-two Virginia acres to his brother James. The next spring, in redbud winter, when spring is yet an unfulfilled promise in the hills, the family left Patrick County and, except for only a few trips back to mark the death of a brother or a sister long after they had been buried, moved away forever.

The great ridge of Pine Mountain, and all the barrier ridges between Kentucky and Virginia, were no easier to cross one way than the other, and eventually Cornelius weaned himself away from the place of his birth. But two of his sons, Elisha and Joseph, would not forget their halcyon youth regardless of the little time they had lived there. They might as well have been living in the old state for all the concern they had for the new one.

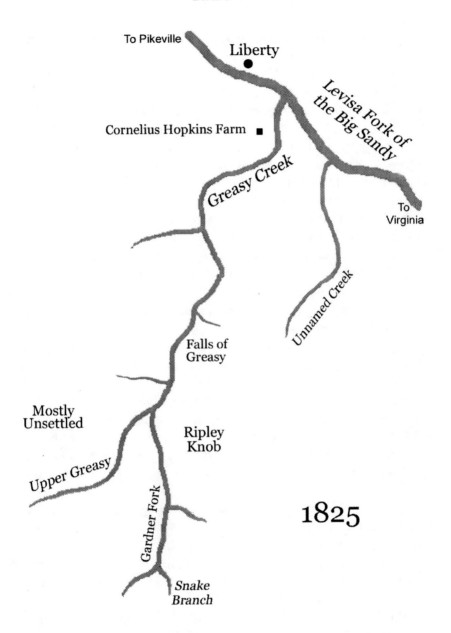

In 1825 the small town of Liberty still exists, but is no longer the county seat of Pike County. Cornelius Hopkins' 50-acre land grant is shown, but there are other settlers living on Greasy Creek as well.

Rissie never told me what the family thought the first time they laid eyes on Kentucky, because the stories she told me were her grandmother's stories and her grandmother was not born when the Hopkinses first made their way through Pound Gap. It was called Sounding Gap then, because of the steady northwest wind that rushes through it, and it later became the eastern terminus of the old Mt. Sterling-Pound Gap Road. The Gap is today, as it was in 1822, the state line, and I drive through it often. Each time I wonder what my ancestors thought when they came there and saw all of Kentucky spread out before them, thick with trees and waiting for white men to conquer them. It is difficult to imagine verdant hills without great scars from strip mining or the unspeakable horror of mountaintop removal. Nor can I imagine trees so large I could not reach around and touch my hands. And although millions of tax dollars have been spent eradicating them, at one time I could not imagine Pike County without abandoned coal tipples and omnipresent slag heaps that smoldered from fires that burned deep inside them.

One of these mounds overlooked the old Greasy Creek camp, as mining towns are categorized for their transient nature, and as late as the 1960's, I could see the steam rising from it every morning as I waited for the high school bus in the morning chill. Summer or winter, the hellish pile burned, and according to Rissie it was worse when the mine was working and more fuel was added to it every day. Although the mine closed in 1929, the slag fire did not burn out until sometime after I graduated from high school in 1964 and moved to Ohio to find work.

That was one of the reasons I discounted my grandmother's stories. How could Pike County have ever existed without the coal industry? What work would people have had if not mining coal? As a child I knew nothing else and I did not know lives could be lived without it in Pike County, although Rissie tried to tell me the Hopkinses once had nothing to do with such work.

When the family first entered Sounding Gap, the view must have been intimidating, but for nearly four decades after that journey, they lived a good life in Pike County. They were prosperous farmers, and used the river often to trade with the North, although their larger

36

business was with Virginia. Elisha also farmed, but he eventually found something more remunerative for his labor.

There were Indians waiting for the family when they arrived at their new home. They had befriended Cornelius while he was alone in the wilderness and Elisha immediately became close friends with the younger members of the tribe. When they gave the family the gift of honey from the bees that worked the blooms of the great poplar trees, it was like nothing they had ever tasted. When Elisha grew up, he began making whiskey from it and, after finding that whiskey was as popular on one side of Pine Mountain as the other, founded a business that would make him rich, at least by standards of the day. He made money, enough to afford more than one family with his earnings.

Elisha had three brothers, two born in Kentucky: Columbus Christopher and John, but he was closer to Joseph, the last child born to the Hopkins clan in Virginia. Elisha was the oldest of the seven children, and looked out for all of them, but Joseph was only an infant when the family drove their oxcarts to Pike County, and much of the way Elisha carried him in his arms and rocked him by the campfires at night as his mother rested from the trip. It would only have been natural for him to love Joseph more, given how he had been so responsible for him at such an early age. Elisha was born in 1815 and when the family came to the wilderness, he would not yet have been ten years old, but charged with the responsibility of making sure his brother was safe.

He never forgot that charge.

By 1860, the entire family had prospered, even though Cornelius still lived modestly beside the river on his original land grant. He was not comfortable with wealth, since he had seen it disappear, and he took few chances with what little he had. His sons were more ambitious, taking so many land grants on the next creek up the river from Greasy Creek that it was named for them. They grew new crops and timbered the inexhaustible supply of trees to make barrel staves and tool handles and other items crafted from the wood. Elisha burned some of the branches for charcoal to filter his whiskey, although the wood he used was a closely kept secret. They floated whole logs down the Big Sandy to the Ohio and occasionally delivered rafts full of dried hemp to make into burlap wraps for the cotton industry.

They decided to raise cotton as well, but Greasy Creek and Hopkins Creek were limited in bottomland. On the western side of Greasy Creek is Little Creek, which feeds into the much broader valley of Shelby Creek, which could support cotton growing. Eventually Joseph, with Elisha's backing, bought property and established a cotton farm for their new venture. It was successful, and during the winter, Joseph borrowed money to buy additional land to expand the farm.

Elisha did not like borrowing money, but agreed with Joseph that more space was needed. In addition, the annual spring flooding of Shelby Creek was usually mild and produced a rich bottomland soil that caused cottonseed to explode into life. The brothers farmed both Hopkins Creek and Shelby Creek until 1857, when Joseph attempted to give his Hopkins Creek property to his brother in exchange for the money Elisha put up for land and seed, but Elisha would not have it.

"It'll still be yours if all your fancy plans go up," he said, and each year the crop grew bigger. In the final, golden summer of 1860, no one had ever seen such a sight when the entire valley, awash in white, revealed itself to the occasional traveler.

Over a hundred years later, at Fishtrap Dam, where Pike County crows had mocked the president of the United States, bird watchers noted that a pair of eagles had begun a nest there and could often be seen diving to the water and lifting back up with a fat, twisting carp in their talons. No one knew when there had last been eagles along the Big Sandy, but all agreed it would have been before coal mining came to the valley and drove them away. In the old texts, there are accounts of eagles and ospreys, as well as herons and other birds that have recently been spotted. On an early morning in 2004, I looked out my front door and saw a dignified great blue heron calmly walking across my front lawn. I thought I was dreaming as it took flight and sailed effortlessly into the early morning mist, but when I later told the office crowd about it, some of them said they had seen it too.

Part of this resurgence in winged creatures may be attributed to the thousands of acres of former mountains bulldozed down for strip mining and the modern reclamation practices required of the coal companies. With little other use for the flattened and unrecognizable land, since almost nothing could be safely built on the unstable soil, many companies created "wildlife sanctuaries," using plants foreign to the region and useless to grazing animals, but able to grow in the nearly lifeless soil. They built large sediment ponds to catch the mud that ran off what remained of the hillsides until the plants took root, and often stocked the ponds with fish after the dirt settled to the bottom. With no one living in those areas to frighten them away and plentiful seed, it is only natural that birds would return. Even the coal companies are surprised at their success, and tout it at every opportunity, but the mountains that once stood so grandly are gone and the only humans to visit these desolate places now are hunters and ATV riders or the occasional hemp farmer who grows his crop now for an entirely different purpose.

If the eagles at Fishtrap were descended from the eagles that lived there in 1860, their ancestors would have had a fright as the summer ended. For as far as the eye could see, Shelby Valley seemed awash in snow in spite of the heat. They may have thought their inner clocks had failed them and they were doomed to spend a cold winter in the mountains, having waited too long to fly south. But they would have been mistaken, for this was not snow blanketing the fields of Joseph Hopkins. It was cotton, acres and acres of it, spread across the valley and up the hillsides as if a huge winter storm had passed through leaving snow drifts four and five feet deep. Only the twists of Shelby Creek, reduced to a trickle in the late summer heat, broke the monotony of the plush carpet.

After a summer of hard work, Joseph awoke one day to see bolls break open, revealing miniature clouds on every stalk, the richest crop anyone in Pike County had ever produced. Soon the family was in the fields, dragging huge sacks that grew progressively heavier as they were filled with the bounty of the year's work and pulling them to Joseph's wagons and sleds waiting nearby. Teams then carried the load to the collection point, where a tripod press had been built to compress the lint that came out of the hand-turned gin and from the work of the women who continued to card the raw cotton by hand. Joseph used some of his previous year's earnings to buy the gin and alleviate the work, but with this crop nearly double what he had produced before, its output was still not enough, and the old cards were pressed into use again.

At the wheel of the gin was George, Elisha's son, whose hands were swollen and bleeding from turning the wheel that turned the machinery to clean the cottonseed from the endless stream of raw cotton fed into it. Across from George, at the other wheel of the gin was his Uncle Lum, Columbus Christopher Hopkins, taking his turn at the slow, monotonous job of transforming the seedy cotton into smooth lint that could be packed tight for shipment. Although the season had not officially begun, riverboats had been dodging sandbars and passing each other up and down the river to collect Joseph's bales and return for more.

It had been a lucky year for the family and spirits were high. George had even higher expectations, for he would soon accumulate enough money to marry.

"How goes it, George?" Joseph asked his nephew as he walked around the wagon after shoveling off another load behind the gin.

"I'm very well, sir," George replied, suddenly putting more muscle into his work until his Uncle Joseph mounted his wagon and drove off for another load. On the other side of the gin, Lum momentarily lost his grip as George pushed the heavy shaft ahead of him.

"Take it easy, boy," said Lum, grinning. "You ain't showin' off for your future daddy-in-law, are you?"

"No, sir," said George, blushing. "Why this ain't hardly no work at all."

"That right?" he asked. "Well, what about them blisters?"

George blushed again but said nothing; his abused hands were not the source of his mortification. Lum had read his thoughts. Each surreptitious glance he took at his first cousin Victoria, with her tiny hands also scratched and bleeding from their work, urged him to greater effort in spite of the fact that his knees buckled each time he caught her looking back at him. The fact that George was in love with Victoria, Joseph's oldest daughter, was the most open secret of the Hopkins clan, and she loved him back. He was twenty and she was seventeen, and everyone in the family was amazed they were still unmarried. They would have been, for people married at a younger age then, had George felt that he could win over her mother as easily as he had won Victoria. He had much to prove to his Aunt Lucinda, not the least of which that he was capable of supporting her daughter in the manner in which she deserved to be supported.

Although it was not unusual for cousins to be smitten with each other while they were children, most grew out of it when they found prospective mates in the other families that populated Pike County. But for George and Victoria, who was now taking her turn carding raw cotton with the other women, and just as discreetly glancing his way, their childhood infatuation never lessened.

This caused no small discomfort for Lucinda, Victoria's mother, who did not like the idea of cousins marrying, and never approved of Elisha's fondness for polygamy. Lucinda worried that her oldest daughter might wind up like Elisha's first wife, Phoebe, who suffered her husband to take two additional wives and start two more families. But Joseph had no such worries; he knew George's heart as well as he knew Elisha's.

"Now, Lucy," he would chide her. "He's not like his daddy, and that's a fact. Hah! There's nobody like his daddy."

At least there weren't any other men like Elisha in his family; his brothers Columbus and John were content with one wife each. Of Cornelius's girls, the oldest, Elizabeth, had died in childbirth years ago, and the remaining sisters, Matilda and Cazey, who was the youngest, afforded Lucinda no more comfort than did Elisha.

Matilda was raising a family with Samuel Robinson, who would not marry her until his Cherokee first wife, who had been taken to Oklahoma with the rest of her nation in 1838, released him with her death. Cazey already had two children and wouldn't identify their fathers. Local gossips had yet to determine which one of the many men she entertained had given her the two young girls that played with the rest of the children in the shade of the trees near Joseph's house.

So Lucinda's worries were not unfounded; the Hopkins clan was lively, fiercely independent, and proud of it, and no one was happier with himself than Elisha, who was strikingly handsome and was said by those same gossips, some envious, to be able to sing the dress off any woman he met. In the newly genteel society of Shelby Creek, where Virginia was still the model to emulate, Lucinda would not talk much about the Hopkinses of Greasy Creek.

"You know George is a good boy," Joseph would argue her. "Name me one soul that's ever had a problem with him. I don't recollect I ever saw him take a drink."

Of course, George had sipped his father's whiskey on more than one occasion and shared a drop with friends when the occasion presented itself, but he had never been drunk, at least in public. Lucinda knew that, and could never offer a rebuttal to her husband, but was always on alert to any change in George's character, although she did allow that his blistered and bleeding hands indicated a willingness to work. But it was yet an unspoken agreement between young George and his aunt that decorum had to be observed. If he were to take Victoria away, she would require a home with cut lumber to repair to. With Joseph's new wealth, simple cabins were insufficient for their improved lot in life.

In spite of her pretensions, Lucinda had to admit that there was a unique charm in the Hopkins family, with the irrepressible Elisha at its head. His laughter was infectious and all the Hopkins children, regardless of their parents, considered him their surrogate father. And all the Hopkinses had arrived to help with the harvest: Lum and his family were there; Cornelius's youngest son John and his family; and all Elisha's children as well, the married girls Elizabeth and Bethina and their husbands taking their turns attacking the cotton fields. Lucinda saw no shirkers in the crowd; all of them picked or ginned or carded or pressed or lifted the heavy bales onto the wagons, and all of them sang and joked as they labored.

There were others, too: the Adkins family helped, since Phoebe, the woman Elisha legally married in 1833, was an Adkins and called in her relatives as well. Her nephew Jesse Adkins was there with his wife of only a year and their first child was on the way. All the girls in the family fluttered around her.

"If it's a boy," young Lucy Cox Adkins said proudly to them. "We're going to name him Henry for Jesse's daddy and his brother." Henry was one of Phoebe's brothers. "But we'll name her Nancy for my sister if it's a girl."

Jesse, thin and rangy, even for his not yet twenty-year-old frame, endured the usual teasing of the men as he took his place in the fields. "Just look at that boy," Elisha laughed. "He wouldn't make a sound runnin' through dry leaves. You know God damn well what he's doin' all night."

Phoebe's niece Clarinda, the daughter of Phoebe's brother Winston, and Clarinda's husband, Zachariah Phillips, were also working, but they would have been anyway, since Clarinda and Zachariah were the best friends of Joseph and Lucinda and, like Elisha, had a stake in the cotton venture. Joseph had offered it to Zachariah when he first acquired the Shelby Creek property, for he knew Zachariah well and knew that he was dependable and honest. Zachariah and Clarinda lived beside the Hopkinses of Greasy Creek, and had bought their 100-acre farm from Elisha's brother John, although the real seller was Elisha, who liked to keep his holdings secret.

Life had been hard for the Phillipses; Clary and Zack had lost a daughter early in their marriage, and then two of their children, twin boys, died of fever after desperate nights of cooling them with spring water and praying for their recovery. When they died within minutes of each other, Clarinda thought she would go mad, with her children lying still and motionless in front of her, their bodies growing cooler with each touch. But Lucinda was with her, and had been there for days, and helped her wash their small bodies to prepare them for the grave as Joseph and Zachariah began building their caskets.

The Phillipses buried their sons beside their daughter in the rapidly-filling first Hopkins cemetery on Greasy Creek, and before a new cemetery was laid off, Zachariah and Clarinda gave up another child to the old burying ground. Francis Marion Phillips, whom Zachariah had named for the great Revolutionary War soldier known as the Swamp Fox, was the fourth of their children to lie in that silent earth. He was buried beside the others, just below Elisha's sister Elizabeth and her stillborn child.

The year before Francis Marion died, Zachariah and Clarinda had another child, and Zachariah named him Joseph, in honor of his best friend. This child would survive the diseases and accidents that took so many young lives and become my great-great grandfather on my mother's side. When she married my father, they completed a circle that even they did not know began nearly a hundred years before.

Other families related to the clan also helped with the crop. The Thackers, Cornelius's in-laws, came to help his sons, and the Robinsons were there. Sarah Robinson, known as Sally in the vernacular, was the matriarch of Elisha's second family. She was also the daughter of Samuel Robinson. She was small and quiet, with long black hair that revealed her mother's Indian ancestry, and had fallen in love with Elisha at the same time as her father became smitten with Elisha's sister. Samuel accepted the arrangement when Elisha took Sally for his bride, since he could produce no certificate legitimizing his relationship with Matilda and called him his brother-in-law "son" with no embarrassment, except, of course, to the eternally chagrined Lucinda Hopkins.

The only in-laws noticeably absent from the field were the Blackburns, kin of Elisha's third wife Mahala Blackburn Cassady, who had disowned her when she divorced her husband and left her two children five years before to came to Greasy Creek with Elisha. The children she bore Elisha were the youngest of his brood.

Although Haley was not much taller than either of Elisha's other two wives, she had a vivacity that made her seem larger than life. With a creamy complexion and nearly blond hair, she was different from Phoebe or Sally, and in any other such arrangement could have demanded primacy over the other wives simply because of her beauty, but she never forced the issue and shared equally in the responsibilities of the family. Both Phoebe and Sally learned to accept her and they were not forced to do so; Elisha made it clear he heartily loved all his women and all their children equally.

At any other time, Lucinda would have been uncomfortable with Elisha's wives and concubines, not to mention his offspring, both legitimate and baseborn on her property, but certain exigencies could not be denied. Cotton farming was labor-intensive work and harvest time was the most backbreaking, so she kept quiet, even when the Indians appeared and quietly took their places in the unsullied snow that covered Shelby Creek.

As Zachariah filled a wagon and headed down the Shelby Creek road to the river, another passed in the opposite direction. Walking beside the team, for he did not like the jolting he would have had in the plank seat, was Elisha himself, and before he could be seen his singing was heard, the valley resounding with his clear baritone:

Oh, the hours sad I left a maid
A lingering farewell taking,
Whose sighs and tears my steps delayed
I thought her heart was breaking.
In hurried words her name I blest
I breathed the vows that bind me,
And to my heart in anguish pressed
The girl I left behind me.

It was Elisha's favorite song, and everyone turned to the great, booming figure that approached the farm. Lucinda often huffed to Joseph that she could not understand why Elisha liked that song so much, since he didn't seem to leave any girl behind him, but Joseph would only smile and shake his head.

"Hallo, the farm!" Elisha bellowed as he came through the gate. "How goes the day?"

Elisha stopped and tied up the team of horses and put his hands on his hips to summon his most fearsome scowl. With mock anger rising, he challenged the assembly: "Why ain't this work done? What on God's green earth has kept you all from finishing this tiddly little piss-ant job?"

At the sound of his voice, his children began to scramble toward him. He looked for his daughter Dorcus, whom he named for his mother, and made a demand of her: "Belle? Belle? Where are you, girl? Break me off a keen switch right quick now. Looks like I've got to tan me some lazy young hides!"

Dorcus, whom Elisha called Belle, as he gave pet names to all his children, made no move to comply. It was a common game Elisha played with his children when he was away for any length of time. It had taken over half a day for Elisha to deliver his load of bound and processed cotton, and he had yearned for them while he was gone.

The children, giggling as they ran toward him, turned away in mock terror as he ran after them and scooped up the youngest, two at a time, and with a measured whack on each tiny set of buttocks, put them down and chased the older ones. Those he wrestled to the ground, rubbing his beard into their faces, and they screamed in glee at the attack.

"All right, enough now," he finally said. "Back to work or there'll be no supper for you tonight." And the children, exhausted from the work that had gone on for days returned to their labors, rejuvenated from the attention of the great man.

Joseph watched this display with a little envy. He wished he could be as unreserved with his own children, but that was another difference between him and his brother. Joseph was more serious, more concerned with the future if something were to happen to him, and he was afraid of showing too much affection to his children should he have to leave their lives. He believed strongly that they had to be prepared for anything that could happen and he had a touch of foreboding about him. He had paid to send his children to school to learn to read and write so that they would be ready for anything in the future, even though he had all girls, except for one son, John Miles, who was also in the group lovingly ravaged by his Uncle Lige.

For Elisha Hopkins, there was no such thing as melancholia, for the future did not exist for him. He lived entirely in the present, or more accurately, in the moment. Strong and wealthy, he did not worry about the future because he knew he could dismiss anything that fate presented him. His enthusiasm for living was legendary and infectious, and Joseph appreciated every moment he spent with his brother.

What is it, Joseph wondered, that makes his women love him so? And his children would walk off the edge of the earth for him.

"The river's up," said Elisha, smiling, as he walked to his brother with the report. "I 'spect it's rainin' up in Virginny. The captain says he can hold off at least another day and take about twenty more bales if we can get them to him."

"Zack has eight on his wagon and we've got six more already pressed now, "Joseph replied, pointing to the growing stack near the tripod. "And we've got a good ten more in the field."

Elisha looked toward the fields and smiled.

"We're going to hit a hundred and twenty bales before this is finished," he said with a broad grin. "A hundred and twenty God damn bales of cotton."

The brothers had indeed been successful; the rains held off and at night the moonlight had illuminated the fields with an uncommon brightness, allowing the family to work until the moon went down without stopping.

Day or night, Elisha was constantly in motion, issuing commands, exhorting the family to work, entreating, encouraging, and mesmerizing them.

"Watch for snakes!" Elisha's voice could be heard in the semidarkness as they worked. "Them God damn rattlers won't come out during the day when it's hot. Put some shoes on."

During the day, he instructed them in avoiding wasp and hornet stings. "Leave those God damn nests alone," he would say. "We'll burn 'em out when the sun goes down."

And on they worked: Joseph's farm produced eighty-six bales the year before and this year Elisha had already taken ninety to the dock at Shelby. "You done good, brother," Elisha said, looking out over the last redoubt of the untouched cotton as the family began its final assault.

"We done good," Joseph corrected him. "I couldn't a done it without you." And after a short pause he said, "And the rest of the family."

"Well, hell, we got more to do," said Elisha. "So let's get this over with and load up that boat. Remember, we've got a feast on Greasy next week. I want Pappy to be proud of us."

"What are you going to fix, Lige?" asked Joseph. Elisha's culinary skills were also part of his reputation.

"Fish, my boy," Elisha replied. "Going to have one hell of a fish fry. Them God damn carp were just floppin' today. Could've reached out and grabbed half a dozen if I wanted to. Scared hell out of the horses when I watered em'. By God, a catfish grabbed Ol' Daisy and tried to drag her in. Took three of us to pull her back out of the water and the God damn cat spit her shoe back at us."

It was a typical Elisha story and he laughed and slapped Joseph on his back before he turned to finding his daughter.

"Belle?" he shouted. "Belle, where are you girl?"

Dorcus came running up to him barefoot, as was almost everyone on this hot afternoon. She was twenty-two years old, and was his right hand. With three wives, it was difficult to prevent jealousy among the women. To stave off any such problems, Elisha had some time ago delegated her to be his plenipotentiary and she was successful at her job. All the women trusted and confided in her; they sensed a special strength in her, a growing wisdom beyond her years. Both Sally and Haley confided in her as if she were their sister, and Phoebe treated her more as an equal than a daughter.

Dorcus's post was one that would normally have been filled by the oldest son, but most families did not have three mothers, and George would soon leave his home to start another with Victoria. Elisha had depended on Dorcas for as long as she could remember, and it was not entirely to her liking. She would have liked to be freer, and was not pleased that her sisters had already begun families and she had yet to have a steady beau or any beau at all. Few of Greasy Creek's swains would have risked the wrath of Elisha Hopkins.

"I'm here, Daddy," she said, as she appeared from the gaggle of women at the carding tables.

"You save me anything to eat, girl?" Elisha had been gone all day and was famished.

"Yes, sir, we got plenty." And she pointed to a table under a tree where the food awaited him. They walked toward it and he whispered to her conspiratorially.

"Anybody been into my jugs while I was gone?" he asked.

"No, sir," she replied. "Just the men now and then."

"Good," he said. "Don't let Cazey have a drop or she'll get drunk and won't be worth a damn." But Belle had already slipped Cazey more than one draught. Elisha assumed as much, but did not ask his daughter to betray her aunt. And besides, the work would soon be over and there would be a grand party on Greasy Creek to celebrate what they had accomplished on Shelby Creek. Then Cazey would be allowed as much to drink as she wanted. With the profit from this year's crop, Elisha could afford to be generous.

For three more days, the family worked in the fields or at the gin or the carding tables or sewing the burlap covers for the bales. Another steamboat, the third to carry Joseph's cotton, arrived to take the last of the cotton and pallets of last year's hemp, dried and sorted for the burlap factories of Cincinnati. The family worked through the nights with the moonrise and caught a little sleep when it went down, only to awaken with the dawn to begin all over again. They no longer noticed the cuts and scratches or the insect bites and they no longer concerned themselves with their swollen hands and aching backs. The rain held off, seemingly as if Elisha had willed it to stay away and they were unimpeded as they stumbled, nearly drunk from exhaustion, through their final chores as the sun began to sink toward the hills.

When the last bale had been loaded onto the wagon, Joseph put his son on the buckboard seat beside him and drove the team down Shelby Creek after he offered his thanks to his family for their labors. In turn, they gathered up their belongings and their children and headed up Little Creek to the buffalo paths that would take them home. The Indians were already gone; they had slipped away as quietly as they came. As Elisha crossed the hill by torchlight from Little Creek to Greasy Creek, the deep blast of the steamboat whistle silenced the night birds that were singing him home, and he knew that his brother had put the last bale on board. Now the family would have something great to brag about to Pappy, he thought. Now they all would be rich.

It had been a good year; the best year of their lives, and nothing on earth could take this summer from them. It was the final justification of Cornelius's gamble when he brought his family here forty years before.

And they would all sleep well tonight; some of them were already snoring as they walked along, anticipating the sweetness of goose down feather beds. Some were so tired they would not wait even for that, and climbed into the haylofts of their barns and fell instantly to sleep.

I do not know to which cabin Elisha adjourned when he got back to the forks of Greasy Creek: Phoebe's, Sally's or Haley's. He would have been proud of all of them, but whoever he slept with that night could have assumed that she had done the best job and his coming to her cabin would be a special reward, so he may have simply eschewed them all and spent the night drinking with his Indian friends; he had done that many times before. My grandmother did not tell me and likely would not have given me that information anyway. I was a child when she told me her stories, and much of what I learned I had to glean from reading between the lines. It was enough for her to admit that Ol' Lige made whiskey and had three wives and scores of children. Any further details would have been a bit too much for my formative mind to absorb.

Nor do I know if the words I gave them here were the words actually said on Joseph's cotton farm that summer. I was not there to hear them and neither was Rissie, for she was not born when they were spoken. But Dorcus was there, and she heard what they said and told my grandmother this story, and my grandmother told it to me. I will not swear that I have repeated it factually; after a century and a half, much could have been lost in its repetition, but I suspect both their spirits would have corrected me if I strayed too far from the truth.

I know this much is true, however: I know that George's aching muscles and throbbing, blistered hands would have reminded him of Victoria's delicate fingers, equally burning from their hard week's work and that he would have gone to sleep that night with his beloved as his last thoughts, as they always were, just as her last thoughts were of him. And I know that Zachariah and Clarinda would have passed by the graves of their children on the way to their cabin and would have paused to tell them that they had not been forgotten during the week their parents were away and that they would never be forgotten. And I know that all the clan would have rested well that night, for they had all been together and they would all be wealthier for what they did, not only in money, but in another currency, one much harder to acquire, but one that cannot be lost as long as a family survives.

But this I will swear to, because I was there when she told it to me, as sleep tugged at my eyelids, as I struggled to stay awake after she had recreated that glorious summer for me one cold winter's night. She had banked the fire and pulled the quilts up to my chin, and I wanted to know that my family, whoever they were, were once as warm and safe and happy as I was at that moment:

"And did they live happy ever after?" I asked her.

"Yes, baby, they were happy," she whispered.

"Happy ever after?"

"For a while they were," she said wistfully, and then she repeated it, as much for her grandmother, whose spirit was also in the room, as for her grandson, who was nearly asleep and had already begun to forget most of what she had told him:

"For a while they were. For a little while."

A Girl in a Doorway

*T*hey had wives and children, the Boys of Greasy Creek, or they had sweethearts, and I had been told nothing that would explain why they left them and went off to war. In school, I read nothing about my secluded region in the Civil War and for the better part of my life I thought little of it. Now I seethe over the omission, for I know that neither my homeland nor my family was immune to the madness that swept the country.

Six men sent their blood down to me over the generations: three Union ancestors, two Confederates, and one Confederate who went over to the Union, and their brothers, their friends, their neighbors. Few men of my family escaped the War and none escaped its aftermath. I could piece together some of their stories, those that my Hopkins grandmother told me, and I could find a few simple facts about the others, but I knew precious little, as my grandmother would have said, about my people.

It was not that I had no other resources to turn to in my youth: the old people of Greasy Creek had the stories inside them, but I did not ask to hear them. My Prater great-grandfather died in 1981 at 101, still alert to the end, and I was his favorite. Yet I rarely thought it necessary to inquire of his knowledge, although on the occasions that I did, his stories tumbled out as freely as Rissie's. I still grieve for what I could have learned about that side of my family at his feet.

But it was not merely my elders who tried to teach me; Greasy Creek has its ghosts, and they also tried to speak to me, but I ignored them too. More than once in my life, I walked into mysteries in that haunted place and walked away without accepting the modest gifts they could have bestowed. One of those times came back vividly forty years after the fact.

On a warm spring day in 1963, over a hundred years after the War began, I drove my car, a newly washed and waxed, vacuumed and polished four-door 1956 Ford with a Mercury engine, up the farthest reach of Greasy Creek with two passengers. Beside me on the front seat was a girl and beside her another boy, making us a combination of three, in search of another girl to round out the number. There was a new Elvis movie at the Pollyanna Drive-In Theater and we wanted to go.

At least that was our excuse.

Aside from mere entertainment, drive-ins at that time were the most acceptable way to be alone with a sweetheart and escape adult oversight. The proper arrangement for such an adventure would have been two couples, a boy and a girl in the front seat and a boy and a girl in the back for the movie, and then to park somewhere, turn up the radio and play the music most accommodating to romance. Two couples would insure at least a modicum of safety for the girls by providing an element of restraint on those prodigal nights.

There was no FM to speak of and the local AM stations would go off the air at sundown, so we would wait until pitch dark for the big stations in faraway cities to come in. Late at night, after listening to all the rock and roll stations, we would surreptitiously turn to WLAC in Nashville, if the ionosphere cooperated, and listen to blues. "WLAC: Away Down South in Dixie," the announcer would say, before he played another anguished wail to lost love, intrinsically Negro in words and rhythm, primitive and earthy, simple but rich, and nothing, of course, our parents would have allowed us to hear.

Such Saturday nights were a weekly ritual, if we had money to afford the admission and chilidogs from the concession stand. Our girlfriends would have demanded at least that much tribute before submitting to a Lover's Lane tryst.

The girl in my car recommended another girl for our entourage, but when we arrived at her house, her mother redirected us up an old dirt road to her own mother's house where our quarry awaited. We bounced through the ruts, alternately covering my fresh wax with mud and dust, until we arrived and found two houses: one a nondescript frame structure with white siding and a swing on the front porch, and the other a weathered, sagging log cabin of what appeared to be two rooms. I could see curtains inside the ancient glass *window and a battered washtub hanging beside the door. Behind the cabin was a garden with a lettuce bed already full, and spring onions growing in neat, straight rows near a trellis heavy with sweet pea blooms.*

We pulled up, and I honked the horn in the usual chivalrous manner for the time, and my objective came out of the cabin to my car. She was wearing a white apron, which seemed incongruous with her plaid shirt tied at the waist, her loose green shorts, and delicate bare feet. Her legs were slightly sunburned, a token of her impatience to get a tan. It was April, and school would soon be out for the year, and I could see wisteria blooming to the side of the cabin, along with a few early butterflies working the blossoms.

"I can't go," she replied to my offer. "Granny's doing her spring cleaning and I gotta help her."

"Your granny lives there?" I asked, incredulously.

"Yeah, her whole life," she said. " She's my great-granny actually. Mamaw lives in the house. Granny's grandpaw built that cabin before the Civil War and she won't live anywhere else. It's still got a dirt floor."

A dirt floor?

"She don't even have juice," she continued. "She's got an old kerosene lamp to read with."

"She lives there even in winter?" I asked. "Ain't it cold?"

"No, it's real warm, and cool in summer, too."

"How old's your granny?" I asked.

"Ninety-one, so it's bound to be healthy for her. You wanna meet her? She tells some really interestin' stories."

"Nah," I said. "We gotta go."

I could sense her disappointment, although I wasn't sure whether it was because she could not go or I wouldn't come into the house.

"You really can't go with us?" I asked again, keeping the despair repressed in my voice.

"Sorry," she said. "But I gotta help Granny. I promised."

"OK," I capitulated. "Maybe next time."

And she returned to the cabin, but not before stopping on the worn threshold of the cabin to turn to us, regretfully, one last time. She waved goodbye, and her white apron, supplied by her Granny as proper dress for a decent woman, fluttered against the redness of her newly tanned legs as she slipped inside. My companions immediately began considering other candidates as I began to turn the car, but something caught my eye in the doorway just vacated.

Someone else was now standing there, another girl much the same age, but with skin deeply tanned, as if it were September and she had worked all summer in the fields. She was wearing a long, plain dress that hid her legs entirely, but not her bare feet. Her dark hair was pulled back severely, and some expression far more abject than disappointment was etched into her forehead. She stood on the doorway for the briefest of moments, her hands fiercely twisting her own white apron and staring intently at me, and then she faded into the darkness of the cabin.

I did not ask my companions if they saw her; they were already debating our next target, and I was not sure that I had actually seen what I thought I did. So I said nothing and soon we were bouncing back down the rutted hollow road to the rest of Greasy Creek until the cabin, awash in lavender and crowned with butterflies, disappeared in my rear-view mirror.

I had forgotten that scene until I stood in front of my Prater great-great-great grandfather's Federal tombstone on the day work began to remove his grave. It all came back to me as I watched the backhoe knock down what was left of the graveyard fence, and when the honeysuckle that covered it fell, something rushed by me, another fragrance, something I had not tasted in years, bringing back vividly the first time I took notice of it outside that ancient cabin in the far reaches of Greasy Creek.

At the end of the day, after the backhoe was stilled and the gravediggers left to return in the morning, I also left and drove back up the hollow I had last visited forty years before. The cabin was gone, along with the frame house that stood beside it. The coal companies had strip-mined the hollow and no houses at all survived, but I knew where the cabin had been. A tiny wisteria vine had pushed back to the surface, as if in memory of the cabin and Granny and all the girls who once walked through her doorway. But that was all that remained, and I wondered if the fragrance that brought me back that day was as sweet a hundred years before I first breathed it that early spring day on that dusty road in 1963.

What had I seen? Was it the ghost of a young woman who had given up her man in that same perfumed air in another April a century before? And how many other wives or sweethearts of Greasy Creek stood in such doorways and watched their men depart, knowing that they might never return? Would they have held their tears or would they have begged, pleaded, entreated them not to go? Who was the anguished ghost who glowered at me? What was she trying to tell me?

It was a sign, an omen; I know that now and I should have heeded it. I should have gone inside that cabin and met that girl's granny. I should have asked her about the cabin, about the man who built it, about the War that came after it was built, about the children who were born there, about the girls of Greasy Creek and if she communed with their spirits as she turned down her kerosene lamp every night and committed herself to the darkness.

But it was the 1960's not the 1860's, and I was driving a 1956 Ford with a Mercury engine, and my interest was in girls without aprons and drive-in theaters on summer nights and blues on an AM radio, and I never went back up that road until it was too late.

Chapter Three

The Boys of Greasy Creek

John Cabell Breckinridge, the youngest vice president of the United States and the man who almost became its sixteenth president, came to Pike County in September of 1861, truly as a fugitive. After losing the election of 1860, he was elected senator by the Kentucky Legislature and went back to Washington in the waning days of his vice-presidency to oversee the certification of the election of Abraham Lincoln and to take his new seat in Congress. For a full term, he sat in the hall he once presided over and attempted to rebind the Union that had been shattered the previous year.

After Congress concluded its business in August, Breckinridge left Washington and returned to Lexington, doubly depressed at what he perceived as his failure to head off the War and his own role in triggering the rush to secession. He had argued sensibly and comported himself honorably, but as his train passed the Manassas battlefield, where the dead offered no valedictory to his efforts, he gave up his last hope of reconciliation.

He had planned to leave office and live out his life as a private citizen, but he had little time to ponder his future. He had barely unpacked his trunks when he received word that federal troops were on their way to arrest him for treason. He then realized that he could no longer be a voice for peace, for men were dying now, and he could not in good conscience turn his back on the spirit that led them into battle. Most awful to him, he knew he helped create that spirit.

With a good friend and two ancient horses, Breckinridge slipped away from Lexington under cover of darkness and rode hard into the mountains of Eastern Kentucky. He had other options; he could have ridden south or west, yet he came to the hills and spent his last three days as a citizen of the United States in Pike County.

There are no highway markers on the road he took to indicate any part of his ride that lonely September night, and the history books say nothing about what he did here or why he came, but he came. There are only a few books written about Breckinridge, who fought more battles than any other Confederate general and was the last and best secretary of war for the Confederacy. Moreover, the South, still enthralled with the magnificent image of a stoic Lee at Appomattox, owes him a greater debt than it knows, for Breckinridge ensured the legacy of the Southern Cause. Without his efforts in the Last Days, the Southern military would have degenerated into guerrillas hiding in the mountains and ruinous years of partisan warfare would have besmirched the birthright of generations of Southern boys. There would have had no great past to mourn for, no grandfather-whispered stories of heroes to honor forever.

But Breckinridge did not know what the gods had in store for him when he came to Pike County. Only recently has history admitted that he came here, as if we are to be given that credit only grudgingly. But I cannot help but believe that there was a reason he made that arduous trek, as if he might have remembered the story of Christ in the wilderness, and prayed for guidance before going on to meet his fate.

A great man came to visit Elisha once, Mammy said . . .

On the night of his flight, Breckinridge followed the Mt. Sterling-Pound Gap Road to Prestonsburg in Floyd County, all the while looking over his shoulder for pursuers. He arrived at daylight, and in spite of his lack of sleep and mental exhaustion, summoned the energy to give a patriotic speech to the new Confederate Fifth Kentucky Infantry, encamped and drilling on the plain behind the Samuel May house. One of the scions of that family was Andrew Jackson May, the occasional attorney for the Hopkins family. May would become an officer in the new regiment, after recruiting heavily from Greasy Creek and he would later form the Tenth Kentucky Cavalry when the Fifth mustered out. Beside him stood John Stuart Williams, known as "Cerro Gordo" for his service in the Mexican War, who would be the commander of the Fifth for its single year of enlistment. Later on, Cerro Gordo would again command the Greasy Creek boys when the Confederacy shrank back to the border of Pike County.

Spontaneous cheers erupted as Breckinridge spoke, and some boys in the new regiment had tears in their eyes as they pressed close to the house for a better glimpse of the man who carried the Southern banner, albeit unsuccessfully, in the last election. They knew he would lead them to victory, and Breckinridge knew full well that when those boys fought, they would be fighting as much for him as for the South, and he fulfilled his obligation well.

Breckinridge was no stranger to Eastern Kentucky, and the fact that he came there for sanctuary meant more to the men arrayed in front of him than would have a visit from Jefferson Davis himself. Not a man among the regiment would have declined the opportunity to storm the gates of Hell if he were leading them. And they would have no fear; the Devil himself would wither under the fierce gaze of Breckinridge's piercing blue eyes.

Like ice on the river, Mammy said . . .

He had not yet grown the great mustache that stirred the boys who fought under him, but the awesome power of the glare was a weapon unto itself, and more than a few of the mountain boys shivered when they looked into his eyes.

That night a small council of war met around the May dinner table, and in response to the entreaties, Breckinridge offered his advice on defending the valley in the coming hostilities. Bottles and jugs appeared repeatedly, including one Jack May proudly attributed to Elisha Hopkins, and the strong smell of a hundred cigars followed Breckinridge up the stairs as he wearily took leave of his retinue and retired for the night. At the top of the stairs he looked out the window at the sea of campfires and thought to himself: they'll never defeat these boys. *They'll never defeat them, but we will still lose. God help them.*

The next morning, with an armed volunteer escort, he went on up the river to the house of the County Judge in Pikeville where another large crowd awaited him. Still exhausted from his flight, and no less miserable, he pulled himself together once more to speak to the crowd and endured another stream of well-wishers before accepting the judge's offer of a bed for the night. For a second night, he could see campfires from his window, campfires of men who would soon be in battle, and in this awful war that had already broken out, he had trouble finding words to say to them. What could he say? They would soon be fighting an enemy unlike any their country had fought before: they would be fighting each other. How could he demonize their brothers, their chums, their fathers? *God help us all.*

Breckinridge's plans were to ride through Pound Gap to Abingdon, Virginia where he would send a telegram to Jefferson Davis that he was joining the Cause. He would then take the train back to Danville, Kentucky where he would enlist as a private soldier in the Kentucky State Guards of Simon Bolivar Buckner. He had enough of leadership and its consequences and he wanted only to do his duty, but he doubted he would be allowed even that small boon.

The thirty-mile trip from Prestonsburg to Pikeville had enervated him and he was more tired than he had ever been in his life, perhaps from adopting a face he did not want to wear, and after raising his glass too many times, he offered his regrets to the assemblage and again retired to his room. He was determined to make an early start in the morning, but when he awoke the next day, another crowd had gathered outside the judge's house, awaiting a glimpse of the great man; and after a speech on the judge's porch and amid the mountains of food offered him and more whiskey and back-slapping, it was too late to continue and he was compelled to spend a second night. By then, everyone in Pike County had heard he was there and nearly all his friends had come to pay their respects. Nearly, but not all, Breckinridge noted to himself. He was by no means vain, but wondered why one of his friends was absent.

The following morning he rose early to make his final good-byes, but was again delayed by admirers before he rode out of Pikeville. Upon hearing word of spies in the local courthouse and Unionists who could threaten his passage, he decided on a different route. He would not continue on the Pound Gap road, but instead would take the more primitive road to Grundy in Buchanan County and then on to Jeffersonville, in Tazewell County, where a telegraph station was in service. He told few friends of his change in plans, and after circling around the town, he descended to the ferry across the Big Sandy River.

On the other side was Lower Chloe Creek, where he crossed the narrow mountain road to Upper Chloe Creek, to find the river again and follow it into Virginia.

His route from Mount Sterling had followed much of what became U.S. 460 in another century, and when he veered off the Pound Gap road for the last leg of his journey, he followed nearly the exact route that 460 would follow when it was created a lifetime later. I yet marvel at the role that road played in Breckinridge's journey and how the reconstruction of it nearly a century and a half later would propel me on my own journey. The fact remains that if my ancient cemetery had not been in its path, I would likely have gone to my grave without rediscovering the family my grandmother had unsuccessfully sought to reveal to me. And like the bits and pieces of bone and wood that came out of those graves, from which we identified only a few of my people, the fragments I remember of her stories allowed me to construct a saga I did not think could have happened here.

The ironies continue to stun me. When Breckinridge finally turned up the Levisa Fork of the Big Sandy, he would ford the river at the place where a dam would rise a hundred years after he was there, and perhaps he may have paused at the very place where one of his vice-presidential successors had spoken at its dedication.

But before he passed through Fishtrap, Breckinridge rode through the remnant of Liberty, where Pike County was born the same year that he came into the world. The county seat was now Pikeville, but Breckinridge knew the history of the tumbledown cabin where the first county court meeting was held. He had a special regard for this easternmost Kentucky county, this arrowhead of the Commonwealth, nearly surrounded by Virginia. It seemed to him the most Virginian of any mountain county, maybe of any Kentucky county, and his friends here descended from the same stock as did he.

On the shore upstream from the hamlet, an unattended ferry was still attached to a huge hemp rope strung across the river. The river was down and the ferryman, having no business to conduct, had gone home. On the other side were wide banks surrounding the mouth of Greasy Creek, which had flowed into the river for eons and where the wheat was chest high and golden in the rich soil that had accumulated there.

The riders, already late in their mission, plunged into water and were soon soaked halfway up their saddles.

Pausing on the other side to remove his boots and shake them out, he looked up Greasy Creek and remembered the powerful liquor that Jack May offered him and that he had not found a match for anywhere he had traveled. In spite of the generosity of his hosts for the past two nights and his own overindulgence, he decided to deviate from his plans. The whiskey would be a good cause to visit, he thought, although there was a more pressing reason: why had Elisha Hopkins not come to see him in Pikeville?

"Hold up, boys," he said to the volunteers who guarded him, all of them armed and sworn to protect him with their lives. "Let's go see Lige Hopkins," he said with a grin. A few of his party did not know Elisha, for they had come from downriver, but they had heard of his liquor.

Elisha's brother Joseph was riding beside Breckinridge at that moment, and among his escorts was Zachariah Phillips, Elisha's nephew by marriage, along with Elisha's young son George, who was attempting to balance Elisha's great Kentucky rifle as he rode one of his father's mares. Breckinridge deemed it strange that these men would have come and Elisha would not. He hoped Elisha was merely busy and that there was no other reason for his absence. Joseph and Zachariah had ridden to Prestonsburg to meet him and George had met them in Pikeville. All three now swore to guard him until he reached Jeffersonville. So why had Elisha, one of his best friends in the mountains, not made an appearance?

"Joseph," he asked, diplomatically. "What kind of year has your brother had? Do you think he would spare a drop for an old friend?"

"Of course," said Joseph, smiling. "Let's ride up Greasy to see him. And if you have the time, sir, you might want to speak to Paw. His cabin's just ahead."

Breckinridge was surprised that Cornelius Hopkins was still living, and when they reached the old man's cabin, he dismounted to shake hands with him. Cornelius was born in Virginia during the Revolution and he still spoke the Colonial tongue that Breckinridge was so fond of, for it reminded him of his Grandmother Black Hat, as they called her for the black bonnet she wore since the death of her husband. She was a Virginian, like Cornelius, and was also a Hopkins, although not of

Cornelius's clan, but still a Hopkins and still of Virginia. The old man seemed like family to Breckinridge.

He took longer than he had anticipated speaking with Cornelius and his wife, but it was worth the time to hear the old man's voice, and after a few final pleasantries were exchanged, Breckinridge mounted his horse and rode on with the riders. At each cabin he passed as they rode up the narrow road that bordered and occasionally went through the creek, they were greeted with cheers and fluttering handkerchiefs. The outriders had informed everyone that John Cabell Breckinridge was on Greasy Creek, and whole families pressed against the fences to see their hero pass.

"Tell me, Joseph," Breckinridge asked with a wink. "How many wives has your brother now?"

Joseph reddened slightly, but answered promptly and with a smile: "Still only three, sir. We may have had some success in discouragin' him from takin' any more."

After rounding a bend, the road began to rise up the mountainside above a waterfall and a wide pool below it that beckoned to the dusty troops. Children were splashing in its crystalline, cold water and diving off a huge flat rock that loomed over it protectively. Breckinridge paused to take in the scene. More than one of the men was struck with a desire to doff his clothes and join the boys who played there.

"I remember well that waterfall," Breckinridge said to Joseph. "I waded in that pool one fine August day, if I recall correctly."

"Yes, sir, you did," Joseph replied. "I was with you. It's right hard to ride by there without jumpin' in, 'specially on a hot day like this."

"Had I more time," said Breckinridge with a wistful smile. "I should like to join those young men." *Would that they should be able to play in those waters until this war is done, and no harm should ever befall them.* It was as much a prayer as a thought, and all the men shared in it without speaking. George had his own memories of the many times he swam in that cold water with his cousins and of a late summer afternoon like this one, when one of them had emerged from the water to sun herself on the rock, her wet dress clinging to the emerging woman inside it. It would be the last image he would remember clearly on his deathbed.

The riders could still hear the children as they approached the forks of Greasy Creek, and the aroma of fried chicken drifted down to them, making them suddenly famished, for none had eaten since hasty breakfasts in Pikeville. As Elisha's farm came into view, the men could see smoke rising from each of his three cabins in the compound. There were women moving smartly through the doors carrying great golden mounds to tables set under nearby trees. Just inside the rough wooden fence stood the great, black-bearded Elisha Hopkins.

He had been waiting for them.

"Hello, the farm!" shouted the visitor, as he wheeled his horse to a stop. "Would a weary traveler find some respite here?"

Elisha smiled and opened the gate.

"Come on in, John Cabell," he said. "It's dinnertime."

"We cannot stay long," Breckinridge said as he entered the compound and dismounted. He smiled as he took Elisha's hand.

"The days are getting shorter and I fear we must travel by night anyhow, but how fare you, my old friend?"

"Tolerable, John Cabell, just tolerable."

Elisha held the gate open until all the riders entered and he returned to his guest.

"You look weary, John Cabell," he said.

"I've seen better days,"

"As have we all," Elisha replied as he tied Breckinridge's horse to the hitching post. There was more in their exchange than what would usually be found in the simple banter of friends, for Elisha looked as weary to Breckinridge as Breckinridge did to Elisha, and they both knew their troubles were not of the body. But they did not speak of it as Elisha led him to the tables.

"We have but little time, Elisha," Breckinridge repeated. "It's a hard ride to Jeffersonville, I'm told."

"Aye, it is," said Elisha. "And you'll not get there this night. Eat now, and stay with me. You can leave at first light and I'll send a guide to take you on a swifter trail."

It took little convincing for Breckinridge and his band to accept Elisha's invitation, especially when his whiskey appeared on the tables. The women scurried back and forth from the houses to the tables bringing fried chicken and green beans and great stacks of cornbread that the riders wolfed down ravenously. Even the young women, who knew even less of politics than the older ones, could not help but be mesmerized with the man whom Elisha brought into his home.

With Breckinridge's permission, the men unsaddled their horses and put them into the pen beside Elisha's barn where feed and water awaited them. By then the sun was fading and some of the men, after their repast, senses dulled by food and drink, rolled out horse blankets on the soft grass under the trees and began to snore. Their host and his remaining guests adjourned to a campfire for coffee as a few of the men picked up their weapons and ordered themselves into the gathering darkness to act as pickets.

Elisha's brother Columbus, who had come down to the forks on Elisha's orders and was waiting in the compound with him, said little as introductions were made and eventually took his leave of Breckinridge and rode back up the creek to his home. Other men of Greasy Creek had come to see the great man in person, but they also said little and departed not long afterward. Breckinridge may have noted their reticence, and with word of bushwhackers on the Pound Gap road, may have wondered how strong the Southern cause actually was in Pike County, but he said nothing.

Sundown was golden and as the shadows crept up the hillside, the women of Elisha's family could be seen standing in the doorways or in front of the cabins, keeping a respectful distance from the affairs of men, keeping at bay the children who contented themselves with chasing moths as they rose from the damp grass and dived toward the campfire flames. Zachariah's wife had been called in to help Elisha's women prepare the meal, and the oldest daughters of the clan had quietly usurped the right to serve the makeshift army at its mess. Dorcus had long been the lieutenant to her father and could make such a demand, and Victoria, her cousin and best friend, could capitalize on Dorcus's power. They were inseparable and often stayed in each other's homes, sleeping in each other's beds, and whispering girlish secrets through muffled pillows. Both of them dreamed of the families they would one day have, and Victoria had already told Dorcus the names of the children she and George would have.

Because of the haste of this occasion, the girls allowed the temporary entry of Elizabeth, Zachariah's oldest daughter, into their clique. Now approaching maidenhood at twelve years old, Elizabeth jumped at the chance to assist them.

"Now don't say nothin', Lizzie," Dorcus warned. "Just take 'em their grub."

The girls said little as they attended to the men, but found excuses to return to the tables until the boards were empty and abandoned for the congeniality of the campfires. Tripods held blackened coffee pots on hangers above the flames and they were emptied rapidly as the women ground coffee beans to replenish them. The girls blushed fiercely when the men took the heavy wooden buckets from them to refill the pots when they were drained, but like the hypnotic swing of a clock's pendulum, their eyes returned to the imposing sight of John Cabell Breckinridge in Elisha's field.

Although Victoria was momentarily stunned by the dusty elegance of the man sitting to Elisha's right, she soon turned her gaze back to her beloved, as George studiously ignored her in his pretense of being a soldier. Elizabeth was as moonstruck as Dorcus, who was a full ten years older, and could easily understand why her cousin had been so flustered when she heard the vice president of the United States was coming to Greasy Creek. She did not really believe such a man existed, in spite of Dorcus's stories of his visits, but Victoria's awe was short-lived.

Victoria never loved anybody but George, you see . . .

As the evening drew on, and more of the riders found sleep under the trees, Elisha gently ordered Zachariah to go to his home just across the creek. Zachariah knew why he was dismissed; he knew his wife's uncle feared that Breckinridge's presence would overcome his argument against going to war and that another night in his wife's arms might temper his recklessness. But he said nothing and took his leave of Breckinridge to walk toward the group where his wife awaited him. Hand in hand they walked into the shadows toward their cabin. Their children, especially Elizabeth, who was just now feeling the stirrings that the older girls had known for years, reluctantly went with them. Soon afterward the other women and their children went inside the cabins, leaving Dorcus and Victoria to sit on the steps of Phoebe's cabin and watch the men by the firelight.

With only Joseph and George attending them, Elisha spoke more freely to his guest: "Well, Senator," he began. "I heard they chased you out of Lexington after you come home. I suppose that means you didn't do much good up in Washington."

"No, sir," replied Breckinridge gravely. "I did not. There was little I could do. There were too many fools beating war drums for reason to have any sway there."

"They say you made a good speech in Prestonsburg," Elisha said. "Did you see my fool nephew Winright Adkins while you were there?"

"I must confess I do not remember, Elisha," Breckinridge replied. "My hand is quite pained from all the grasping it has done in the last few days and if I met him I did not take notice."

"Well, he ain't much to look at," Elisha said. "But the God damn fool believes he has wings to fly. He was one of the first to sign up when Jack May came up here recruitin'. I heard they elected him Sergeant. He was wild as a buck when he left. Nothin' would do him but to leave home and him with a big family. He'll get his sorry ass shot off yet."

Elisha poked the fire and called out to Dorcus for another jug.

"Belle," he shouted to one of the cabins. "Bring us another one, girl. It's going to be a long siege tonight."

Breckinridge could see one of the figures in the twilight jump at the order and rush into a cabin. Presently, she emerged with a small jug, enough for two or three men. Breckinridge took notice of her as she walked deliberately toward them.

"Could that be your daughter Dorcus?" Breckinridge asked when he saw the willowy, dark-haired young woman materializing from the shadows. "She's grown into a woman."

"That's Belle, all right," Elisha replied. "I believe she's still struck on you."

Breckinridge was flattered and could see her stealing glances in spite of her downcast eyes as she neared him. He smiled at her as she approached, and she was certain he could hear her heart pounding.

"Good evening, Miss Dorcus. It is good to see you again." Breckinridge spoke. Then he added: "Or is it Missus now?" Her scarlet face turned even redder.

"How-do, sir," she said, with a slight curtsy as she handed the jug to her father. "It's still Miss," she said breathlessly.

She waited for more instructions from her father, but he dismissed her with a glance and she retired quickly to the darkness enveloping the valley.

"Belle's too headstrong to marry," said Elisha teasingly, as his daughter was still within earshot. "She's too much like me; she scares off all her beaus."

Victoria was waiting for her as she returned to the group, and Breckinridge could hear their giggles as he spoke: "You're to be complimented, Elisha. She's a handsome woman. You'll have to fight off her suitors yet."

And he smiled at her . . .

For a while, the conversation was light: they spoke of hunting trips in times past, of fish fries on the river bank at the mouth of Greasy Creek, of hoedowns and pretty girls and chasing the moon on horseback, fueled by the liquor only Elisha could have produced. Breckinridge remembered those times as the last jug was passed around.

But unlike the other men, George had not taken a drop, in deference to his Aunt Lucinda, whom he knew word would get back to if he did. But he was fighting sleep like a drunken man, and still desperately clutching Elisha's long rifle. The enormity of the moment had exhausted him; the solemn responsibility of protecting the man who almost became president of the United States weighed heavily and not even the close presence of Victoria distracted him. His fingers were nearly white as he gripped the ancient weapon, the one his father had given Elisha, the one Cornelius had brought with him from Virginia.

"George!" Elisha spoke sharply. "Wake up!"

He sprang to his feet at his father's voice.

"Take the gun in the house," he ordered. "You'll get the powder damp out here."

"Yes, sir," George replied.

"Tell Aunt Sally to fix you a bed in her house. You'll pitch into the fire if you stay up any longer." Elisha, in deference to his sister-in-law, would always order George out of the house when Victoria stayed over with Dorcus.

With George's departure, only three men now sat around the fire: Elisha and Breckinridge on cane-bottom chairs to one side and Joseph on a log across from them. Joseph could see the intense blue of the great man's eyes in spite of the firelight.

There was more polite talk: of steamboats on the river, of the railroad Breckinridge had started to build, but inevitably the conversation turned to war. Joseph asked Breckinridge what he thought the war would do to the cotton market. Cotton was still trading, Breckinridge told him, but he was confident the business would soon be interrupted.

It was not good news, but it was also what Joseph expected.

Breckinridge could sense a certain tension between Elisha and his brother. Asking about the cotton market was a way to turn the conversation to the War and Joseph needed Breckinridge to support his entreaties to his brother.

When Virginia seceded, it was all Elisha could do to make his family stay home as young men made their way to the recruiting stations that sprang up in the Virginia counties nearby. Many boys had already answered the mother state's call, and now with Kentucky forming its own regiments, Elisha was rapidly losing ground. He expected Zachariah Phillips to be the first of his family to don a uniform.

Zachariah was only a nephew, married to the daughter of Phoebe's brother, but he was still under Elisha's sway and more impatient than Joseph to go. In spite of his ploy, Elisha did not expect him to return from Virginia after he delivered Breckinridge to Jeffersonville. When Jack May began recruiting, bands of Greasy Creek boys signed up, and almost daily one or two could be seen striking out to enlist. Zachariah announced his intention to follow them, but Elisha had some success in holding him back.

"Look at your children, boy," Elisha had demanded. "Who's going to feed them while you're gone? Who's going to feed them if you get your God damn brains blowed out?"

Up to now, it had been an effective argument.

Then there was George, Elisha's oldest son, who agonizingly watched his chums depart and endured their taunts as they rode by him. Elisha was successful in restraining George, not only because of his absolute intimidation of his son, but because he pointed out that Victoria's beauty would not be unnoticed by the boys who stayed home.

That was the best strategy he could have used, but George was still amazed that his father would allow him the privilege of escorting Breckinridge to Virginia.

But it was Joseph who worried Elisha the most. Joseph had another cotton crop coming in and would not leave prosperity so easily; Lucinda valued it too much and he knew he had an ally in her. But Elisha knew there were stirrings in Joseph's heart that he could not combat much longer. Indeed, he ultimately did not expect to stop any of them. All his boys were hearing a siren call and he feared what would happen when they finally succumbed.

For a year he had listened to their arguments and countered them as best he could. He knew that Lum would join the Union but John would listen to him and stay out of it. He knew Zachariah was fiery and gloried in his North Carolina grandfather's tales of the Revolution. Zachariah saw this war as a second fight for the same principle and desperately wanted in on it before it was over. George had the typical stupidity of youth, Elisha thought, but he was still in thrall to his father, and would not defy him.

But Joseph was different; his oldest brother was serious and contemplative and considered himself more a Virginian than a Kentuckian. Joseph had never been the same since Virginia seceded and Richmond became the capital of the Confederacy. Elisha's rhetoric was strong, but he knew that only the success of the cotton farm kept Joseph bound to him.

Elisha knew that sheer will had its limits, but he told his friend in detail that night why he would fight against the coming war. As the whippoorwills retired from their evening songs, Dorcus could make out most of what her father said.

"I want no part of this thing, John Cabell," Elisha said grimly. "I'm not goin' to let my boys go."

Breckinridge said nothing as he continued.

"One of my fool girls married a crazy man and his brother's already started a God damned Union militia over on the Tug. They're out there somewhere plunderin' as we speak."

"The boys want to go, no doubt," said Elisha, looking at Joseph, who would not return his fierce gaze. "I can see it in their eyes and they can't see beyond the end of their noses, but they don't need to be traipsin' out of the hills to fight somebody else's war. It'll come here soon enough."

"I fear you are right, old friend," said Breckinridge. "But how do you propose to stay out of this thing? There are regiments forming on both sides. Eventually they will clash."

"I know that," Elisha replied. "But I'd just as soon watch it from a distance."

"Look here," he continued. "We're on the border of two countries now, and we're goin' to be fought over. The South can't get across Pine Mountain so easy and the North can steam up the river anytime it wants to. The South can't supply its armies over here and when they come up, they'll eat us out of house and home, and right soon at that."

Elisha looked around as if the columns in gray were already at his gate.

"That's goin' make a lot of folks mad. They support the South and they supported you, but the South can't help them here.

"I been to Cincinnati and I seen the river covered in steamboats. I seen factories by the dozens, broad farmland all the way to the Lakes, and a hundred thousand farm boys lookin' for somethin' to do. They can bring all the men in here they want to and the South ain't got no way to get her boys across those ridges except by foot. No powder, no shot, nothin' to eat; how can she expect to win?

"What ain't already joined over in Virginia will soon join up, and ever county over there'll be stripped bare of men and fodder this winter. It's a hard enough job as it is to raise a family. How they goin' do that when they're dead? Who's goin' to feed their children. Fools! All fools!"

He shook his head gravely and stared at the fire.

"There ain't no good for us in this war, John Cabell," Elisha said. "No good."

So this was why Elisha had not come to Pikeville, Breckinridge thought. He would not want his family to assume that such a visit implied support. And he knew Elisha spoke the truth. Of all the men who would rise to the Southern banner, only a few could see the consequences, and Breckinridge was one of them. Elisha, obviously, was another.

"I agree with you, Lige," said Breckinridge. "But you will understand that I no longer have a choice in this matter."

"I see that, John Cabell," Elisha replied. "I do. But you know that I can't let my boys go. I got three brothers and one son and none of them had nothin' to do with startin' this war."

"But, Lige . . . " interrupted Joseph.

"No 'buts' about it, Joe," said Elisha quickly. "I know what you're goin' to say: 'We're from Virginny, and she's done seceded.' That don't matter. She'll lose; they'll all lose."

"But it's our duty," Joseph pleaded. "Virginia had a right . . . "

"To do what?" Elisha demanded of his brother. "To kill herself? Hell, the God damn city of Washington is on her doorstep. Do you think ol' Abe Lincoln is goin' to let a new country set up under his nose?"

Joseph said nothing; he had too much respect for his brother to argue further, and deep inside, he knew his brother was right.

Elisha turned to his guest apologetically.

"I'm sorry, John Cabell," he said. "You got to do what you got to do, but you know very well you ain't goin' to win. They got big states up north. Big states: New York, Pennsylvania. Any one of 'em has more money than the whole South rolled up together.

"This is the worst thing that has ever happened to this country, and you know it, too."

Breckinridge was silent as he spoke, but after a moment, he nodded. Elisha's logic was nothing more than he himself had preached to no avail.

Elisha turned away from his friend and looked up at the fire and then to the sparks rising into the clear sky. It seemed to Elisha that tonight was much like the Indian wakes he had attended, only worse, since it was for his family he was grieving. He spoke again, this time more softly:

"Last summer, I saw something. I had a vision. I saw what this war is goin' to do to us. I saw it as surely as I can see those stars. I saw death and tribulation. It'll come; I know it will, and I won't let my boys be part of it."

And he turned again to his guest. His tone was still soft, but firm and strong as the mountains he was so much a part of.

"I am your friend, John Cabell," he said. "And I always will be, and I have no quarrel with you. But you must understand why I feel this way."

71

Breckinridge did not reply right away, but sighed, and after a moment he spoke in a far different tone than he had used for the crowds as he made his way to Elisha's farm: "I'm going to Virginia," he said. "To tell President Davis that I am safe, but returning to Kentucky. I shall enlist as a common soldier; I have a duty but I want no truck with leading men again. I failed to prevent this war and I should expect no greater success prosecuting it. I truly understand you, sir, and I take no offense."

Elisha looked at his friend and saw the sparkle had retreated from his bright eyes. His burdens were great, Elisha thought, and he will have many more.

"Jeff Davis will never allow you a lowly role," Elisha said. "You know that better than I do, John Cabell. He needs you and before this war is over you'll be a general. You may have to do even more; I don't know what, but it will come for you and you will accept it."

Elisha put his hand on Breckinridge's shoulder and spoke again:

"I ain't much of a prayin' man, but I will pray for you. Now you're tired and you need your rest. The women made you a bed in the house."

Breckinridge shook his head.

"I appreciate your kind offer, Lige, but by your leave, I'll stay out here." He looked at the men in childlike positions of sleep, some with hands crossed over their breasts and some on their sides with their heads resting on their hands, clasped palm to palm like children at their prayers. He could foresee the nights ahead of him among such men and he caught his breath thinking of the days to come when many of them would never rise from such postures.

"This ground will do splendidly," he said with a slight twinkle in the piercing blue eyes that marked the man and so enthralled Elisha's daughter.

"I suspect I will be sleeping on many such fields from here on," he continued, with a wry smile. "I should soon enough accustom myself to it. I trust you will not take offense if I decline your hospitality."

"I take none, sir," Elisha said. "However, I believe Belle will if you would not take a pillow for your head.

"Belle!" he shouted to the darkness. "Bring that embroidery you been workin' on all this time."

Dorcus felt as if someone had flung a bucket of cold water over her when she heard her father. After all this time, John Cabell Breckinridge had returned and she would actually have the opportunity to give him her present! She dashed into the cabin to retrieve it from it hiding place under her bed. It was a small pillow she had begun years before. It had been wrapped in a quilt and she would never allow anyone to see it, even when she would accumulate an occasional piece of thread to make into the flowers that adorned it. It had been intended to be a gift to her first beau, until she met John Cabell years before, and she was trembling like a schoolgirl when she approached him.

"I thank you, Miss Hopkins," he said as their eyes briefly locked as he rose to accept her gift. "I shall cherish this as long as I live."

Giddier than twelve-year-old Elizabeth Phillips would have been, she turned and dashed back to the cabin and where she and Victoria sat on cane-bottom chairs on Phoebe's porch and watched until Phoebe called them inside. He saw her Uncle Joe shake hands with the man who had been the one constant ideal of manhood in all her dreams and then take the seat Breckinridge had vacated. She watched her father walk with the great man to the edge of the trees and saw Breckinridge roll out his own blanket. She strained her eyes to see if he would really rest his head on her pillow and was ecstatic when he did. She saw her father return to the campfire, where he would sit with his brother until dawn streaked across the mountains.

She watched over him all night . . .

Victoria eventually slipped into bed and Dorcus sat alone at the window of her mother's cabin, drifting in and out of sleep, half dreaming of things she knew she would never have. She would awaken now and then as the pickets came in to rouse up their replacements or a hoot owl would punctuate her dreams with his questions. It did not seem long before the first roosters crowed outside Elisha's henhouse and awakened her. The cabins were already stirring and Phoebe was rolling out biscuits on the table by the fireside.

From her window she could see the men feeding their horses and pouring coffee from the pots Elisha had filled before they got up. She could smell bacon frying as her Aunt Haley joined the rest of the women to take the first round of breakfast to the men now moving around the compound, preparing for the day's march. Although she ventured out with her mother to attend the men who waited respectfully for her offering, she said nothing and returned to the cabin door as the riders gathered.

From out of the mist, one of her father's Indian friends materialized with his horse as the skies lightened sufficiently for the shapes of the mountains to become clear. He could see the young man with hair as dark as her own nod as he received Elisha's instructions. After the men were all mounted, Elisha walked over to the gate and opened it, waiting for them to ride through.

But before he left, Breckinridge came over to the cabin, leading his horse with one hand and tipping his hat with the other. The tiny pillow was under his arm.

"Thank you again, Miss Hopkins," he said, his flashing eyes again locking with hers. "I don't recall sleeping on a more comfortable bed." She could barely force a smile, for she knew she would never see him again. He mounted his horse and tipped his hat to her as he rode out of the compound and Elisha solemnly closed the gate. Even in the dim light, she could see her father's great body heave as he threw the latch and sighed. In a moment, Breckinridge and his riders disappeared into the early morning.

She never saw him again . . .

I often wish I knew more about the other men who rode off like Breckinridge and his riders into those daybreaks of so long ago. I know a few facts about them: their names on federal censuses, deeds to the land they bought and sold, marriage licenses, and the occasional other document that gave me some insight into their lives. But I was *told* little about them if they were not part of Rissie's stories.

Of the boys of Greasy Creek, I know most about four of them: Elisha, Joseph, Zachariah, and George, and only two of them passed down their blood to me. There were five others who gave me their bloodline, five other soldiers of the War, and I wish I knew more about them, but I had no Ariel to whisper their songs.

There was Ezekiel Prater, who was a good soldier and never missed a muster roll, even though the Union's Thirty-ninth Kentucky Mounted Infantry was plagued with desertions. His best friend was Henry D. Adkins, of Phoebe's family, who served with him and recommended the land on Greasy Creek that Zeke eventually bought and on which he was buried with Henry at his feet.

Ezekiel was not living on Greasy Creek then, but Henry came to meet Breckinridge that night, along with David Coleman and Robert Damron, who both joined the Thirty-ninth with Henry. Robert was a wild young man from Little Creek who often took the buffalo paths to Greasy Creek because he thought the girls there were the prettiest he had ever seen. Every year he would join the Hopkinses to pick cotton and to woo their daughters unsuccessfully. When Robert joined the army, he kept his wild ways and was once court-martialed for one of his youthful escapades, but he saw so much horror in his service that he later turned to the cloth and became one of Pike County's most beloved preachers. He founded the Greasy Creek Old Regular Baptist Church on the cemetery overlooking Elisha's field, the cemetery that Zeke would give his name to and where the congregation would meet in summer for a hundred years afterward.

Over in Virginia, a young John Riley would answer the drumbeats to sign on with a Confederate regiment, but would flee as soon as his enlistment was over and come to Pike County to join my other ancestors in the Thirty-ninth Kentucky. He hoped never to return to Virginia, but eventually he did battle there against former Confederate comrades in spite of his prayers.

These men were my Union ancestors, four of them, although one, it must be said, began as a Confederate. My two Confederate ancestors were James Roberts, Jr., who lived just above Joseph's farm and whose grandfather was killed by Indians in Virginia just after the Revolution, and Zachariah Phillips, whose grandfather served in it. They would both join Jack May's Tenth Kentucky Cavalry during one of the bitterest winters of the War, along with Joseph. No fife and drum corps heated their blood when they enlisted, but to them their duty was no less important than it was to my Union people.

One way or another, they were all the boys of Greasy Creek, and they all had their reasons for the choices they made. Like Elisha, I take no side and make no judgments, except one: that I was woefully neglectful of learning their stories and I cannot repeat all of them here. I wish I could. I owe them that, for they all met again on a bright fall day in Virginia in a place where creatures had come for salt for a million years, and if any one of them had killed any other one, I would not be here to tell even the few stories that I can. For that I am thankful, as thankful as Elisha was when all his boys came back after escorting John Cabell Breckinridge into history.

For a while, Elisha may have thought his vision was false. He may have thought he could keep his family together, but within a month, Zachariah said goodbye, leaving a heartbroken Clarinda, to ride north and join the Thirty-fourth Virginia Infantry, just forming in what would later be Unionist West Virginia. Elisha assigned Dorcus the task of protecting his family until he returned, if he did.

The following spring, a flood wiped out most of Joseph's cotton crop and a searing drought followed to stunt what little remained. By the fall of 1862, still owing over a hundred dollars on his land, he had only enough cash for the interest and had to sell his teams to raise that much. When he arrived at the dock in Pikeville with a fraction of what he had produced in years before, he was ordered to take an oath to the United States or he would not be allowed to sell what little he had produced. He refused and at gunpoint his cotton bales were confiscated, with some of them sent downriver immediately to profit the Union officer who took them. But before daylight the next morning, the remainder went up in flames as Joseph watched, soaking wet, from the other side of the river as the bright life he once led lifted up in smoke into the darkness.

A few months later, he signed on with the Tenth Kentucky with Zachariah when Zack transferred to the new regiment, and soon there were few boys left in Pike County to choose sides. When Zachariah and Joseph departed in the dead of winter, Elisha gave them each a bottle of his whiskey to keep them warm. After they left, he took out another bottle and drank it entirely to the lees.

Only George was left, but that was only for a while. "Why can't I go, Pappy?" he asked his father. "Jesse's already gone and he's younger than me." Young Jesse Adkins had already joined the Thirty-ninth, following the lead of his older brother, Henry D.

George's protests carried no weight with his father, especially since George had changed his allegiance since Breckinridge's visit. "Now you're a Yankee?" Elisha demanded. "I remember you dying to join up with Breckinridge."

But George had legitimate reasons to join the Union. With the depredations of roving gangs pretending to be partisans of either side, as Elisha had predicted, and with the Confederacy unable to protect Pike County, as Elisha also predicted, George eventually boarded a steamer to the Union recruiting station down the Big Sandy in Louisa. On the way, he walked through the remains of Cornelius's homestead, burned by renegades, and continued to tell himself that he had no choice as he took the oath and donned a blue uniform. A stunned Victoria swore she would never speak to him again, and Dorcus, to whom Elisha had now assigned another fatherless family, would not attempt to broker a peace between them.

Only Elisha's youngest brother John would fear him enough to stay out of the War. Elisha could point to that as a victory when it all ended, although there was little else he could be proud of. The Boys of Greasy Creek had begun their journeys, and in the end the magnificent blue eyes of John Cabell Breckinridge may not have been much the reason at all, although it remained the only bright memory young Belle had of those times and the most indelible image she passed on to the great-great-grandson she would never meet.

"What color eyes did Mammy have, Mamaw?" *I asked her as we sat in the swing on her back porch and visions of soldiers and sweethearts swirled through my head.*

"As dark as night, my baby," she said to me, smiling. "Just like your own sweet eyes."

I had always believed my eyes came from the Praters, whose eyes and skin were dark, where the Hopkinses had much the opposite features. I had thought the reason I did not share the blue eyes of my father, my grandfather, or great-grandfather, was that my mother's genes simply overpowered my father's, but I may have been wrong.

Maybe the Prater genes were pushed aside as well, and maybe Dorcus sent her genes down to me somehow. Maybe the awesome, inexpressible devotion she had for her ghosts was ultimately rewarded, and they gave her the power to conjure the future as well as the past.

Maybe she was Ariel.

And maybe she knew that her eyes were the only things she could give me that I would not cast away.

Chapter Four

The Girls They Left Behind Them

By the third summer of the War, most of the boys of Greasy Creek and most of the boys of Pike County, those who would see the elephant, had joined up. None of them had ever been soldiers, nor did they know what awaited them outside the coves where they grew up, but they all hoped to return as heroes, regardless of the side they had chosen. For the most part, all of them were impatient as they said their good-byes to their families; impatient for adventure, impatient for honor, or just impatient to see what they had heard about or read about, if they could read, in the newspapers that made their way into the hills. In large groups or small groups or sometimes alone, they left their homes, their sweethearts, their mothers, or their wives and children.

Although the early enlistments were largely Confederate, the victories of Ohio Colonel James Garfield and his enlightened administration of the Big Sandy Valley had won over many who were teetering on the brink of joining the Rebellion. Some of those boys went north on steamboats to sign up in Union regiments in Ohio or Indiana early in the War, or joined the Kentucky Union regiments when they formed later. Some boys went into Virginia and joined the early Confederate regiments forming there or later joined the Kentucky Confederates. Sometimes, they crossed paths with boys from Virginia going the other way. Either way, by 1863 the die was largely cast.

Many Eastern Kentucky Unionists joined the Fourteenth Kentucky Infantry, but most signed up with the new Thirty-ninth Kentucky Mounted Infantry, barely a year old. A few took their own horses when they joined the men in blue, largely to keep them from being stolen if they were left behind, but if they joined the Confederacy, they always took their own, if they had them. A horse guaranteed assignment to a cavalry regiment, which was not only a more dashing organization, but one less footsore as well.

The Fifth Kentucky Infantry CSA, which had been forming when Breckinridge came to Pike County, had already mustered out after a one-year enlistment, but in its place the new Tenth Kentucky Cavalry had been formed with the old Fifth as its nucleus. In both those regiments were Pike County boys, boys Elisha had seen grow up, and now they were gone, some never to return. They had ridden out of Greasy Creek for the last time and some had already been buried, although few had died in any trappings of glory. More commonly, they had drawn their last breaths while covered in sweat and vomit in distant camps where cattle or deer grazed, before the armies turned quiet pastures into clattering cities of mud and filth.

In his mind, Elisha marked them when they left and when word came of their fate he was not surprised, since he had seen them all depart long before the drums sounded. He told almost no one but Breckinridge of his vision, and hoped against hope that what he had seen was false, that what was revealed to him in the faces of his family and friends that last glorious summer the family had gathered on his farm would not come to pass. He told his Indian friends, of course, for they understood those things, but he told no one else until long after the War had ended, and then only Dorcus would hear of what he had seen at his fish fry in 1860.

And now the prophecy was being fulfilled.

As he expected, John did not go, in spite of Lum's enlistment in the Thirty-ninth and the entreaties of John's brother-in-law, Andrew Francis, who was serving in the same regiment. John had married Andrew's sister Elizabeth in 1854, almost a year after Andrew married Elisha's daughter Elizabeth. Such dual marriages often doubled familial connections, and for years Andrew was a full-fledged member of the clan. But the Francis family was fervently Unionist and Andrew's brother, "Yankee Bill," had formed a Union militia soon after South Carolina seceded, and was already harassing Southern sympathizers.

Andrew rode with him for a while and Elisha banished his son-in-law from Greasy Creek forever.

As the War progressed, the great family reunions of which Elisha was so proud were abandoned because of the rift in his family. The last time they had all gotten together, in 1861, politics had intruded so viciously into the gathering that Cornelius himself had broken down in tears. Elisha banished them all with food still on the table and the same day began building a house for his parents at the forks of Greasy Creek, where he could watch over them. He completed it in the fall of 1862, and it was none too soon.

As soon as the new place was finished, he moved Cornelius and Dorcus away from the river, away from the land where Cornelius had built his pioneer cabin and wrought a life from the wilderness forty years before, away from the place where Elisha and his brothers and sisters had grown up, away from the memories of fish fries and happier days, and the ancient homestead was finally abandoned. Roving bands of marauders began to occupy it, until one such band settled in for the night and was attacked by another, and the cabin was burned down.

It was the last straw for George, who swore vengeance on both sides, and picked the Union as the army that could best protect the family, although Victoria never understood his reasoning. None of the Hopkinses expressed any desire to rebuild Cornelius's cabin, at least not until the War was over, but by then no one wanted to return to the river.

John had two infant daughters when the War began, and even without Elisha's entreaties not to go, he could see what was happening to other Pike County families. After a few half-hearted attempts to convince his older brother, he no longer argued with Elisha about joining up, although he kept himself armed, with a rifle and a pistol always handy. More than once, he had to leave home when Union or Confederate "recruiters" came into Greasy Creek looking for men to press into service. The Indians would warn Elisha they were coming and he would send John and George to the top of Ripley Knob, where the cabin stood that he and Joseph built when they were boys, and they hid out until the gangs left Greasy Creek.

After George joined up and then deserted for the first time, he came back to the cabin under cover of darkness, and his mother brought him food until Elisha ordered him to return. Elisha had tried to keep his impetuous son from joining in the first place and George had made his choice without his father's blessing. Nevertheless, Elisha did not want him to see him hanged as a deserter.

The prospect of adventure for the boys of Greasy Creek had diminished considerably from the early days of the War, when the War in Pike County was still more political than military, and some of them had come to sorely regret their decisions. It was not merely the possibility of death in battle that men feared, for indeed there had been few so far, but the specter of death by inglorious disease, of which there had been many, frightened them even more. After all, they thought, you could kill a man who was trying to kill you, but you could never kill an enemy you could not see. The most horrible way to die was by dysentery, and when a soldier returned from leave and asked about an absent comrade, he would often receive only the simplest reply: "the shits." There was nothing left to say.

But as much as the men suffered, an equal and often heavier burden was placed on their wives and children. Greasy Creek had not comprehended this war when it began, and neither had the nation, for both sides felt it would be short-lived. At first, only the most reckless young men had left home to fight, and family men saw little reason to get involved. But by the second year, when it became apparent that the War would go on, many men took stock of the situation and began questioning whether they could stay home and still be men. By 1863, the lines had been drawn, and except for women and either very old or very young men, Greasy Creek was nearly deserted.

It would not have been unusual for someone to ride up the creek that year and see not one strong male frame anywhere in the fields, and not just because they were hiding from "agents" who would shoot anyone who refused to ride out with them. Sometimes, men could get passes from their regiments to put out or harvest crops, but they would soon return to the fighting and they were rarely there to tend what they had planted. Without the experience and the labor of the men, there was no abundance in any mountain farm, and soon enough, the forest began reclaiming fields that had been so laboriously wrested from it years before. Even the boundaries of the farms began to disappear as the split-rail fences that marked them were consigned to firewood, either for a soldier's campfire or for the hearths of the cabins, but there was little stock to keep penned anyway.

Because they had to, women picked up the slack, and took on the responsibilities their men once treasured as their domains: plowing, hunting, fishing, settling disputes within the family, slaughtering their animals, even repairing or making shoes, if shoe leather were available. Too many of the cattle had been sold or rustled for there to be any hides left for making shoe leather, and the lambs, from which soft, warm gloves could be made, disappeared soon into the War. The lack of meat took its toll on the families, and wild game began disappearing as well. The solid fare of the mountaineers was reduced to subsistence, and hunger stalked many of the families. By the end of the War, some of them measured success by the number of children that did not die during the dark years.

The women were already responsible for most home remedies, and they learned more about the art of doctoring without store-bought medicine by consulting with the Indians, who had been largely ignored in the new society that was forming before the War. The Indians had always lived on much less than the white settlers, and now their skills were in demand. A few of the Indian boys, none of whom remembered what had happened in 1838, had gone to the Confederate side, despite the orders of the elders to stay home. But there were old scores to settle with blue-jacketed soldiers. Now for the first time for many, both white and Indian women had reason to associate. And after the crops were put out in the spring of 1863, women and children of any heritage had nearly quit looking down the Greasy Creek road for their husbands and fathers to return.

The redbuds still bloomed, and the dogwoods and sarvis trees still burst open for Easter, but there was little joy in spring . Neither did the churches offer much comfort for their flocks. There was too much work to do for the women and children to spare the time away from their fields, especially at harvest, by which time the women had learned to pick up guns to protect their crops or their livestock. And there was little a preacher could say to a divided congregation anyway, as he would often find himself preaching to one side of the room and then to the other as the families sat with other families whose men served in the same regiments. Little was said when the families marched out, and fights between the children would break out in spite of their mothers' orders to say nothing.

For a country of farms, there were few farmers left, and even the sounds of Greasy Creek were different. A traveler would rarely be greeted with the hissing of a goose, the once omnipresent sentinels and protectors of mountain cabins. Few geese remained by 1863, and those that did were doomed to an abbreviated life, for if they were not stolen, the families had no choice but to kill them for meat to prevent their loss to other families. The neighing of a horse often brought alarm, for it was the harbinger of riders. Most of the horses were sold or stolen by 1863, often by foragers who fancied a stud or a mare for themselves as much as for the battalions they supposedly served, and a farm was blessed if there was still a mule to plow with.

Thieves plagued Greasy Creek, which was close to the river and to the Grundy road, and gunfire often erupted when families defended with their lives the little bit of foodstuffs they had managed to cache for the winter. What was the better end, they thought: to die protecting their homes or starve to death when the snows came? But the armed gangs that ravaged Greasy Creek, and every other Pike County hollow, had no concern for the families they robbed. They themselves would have starved, had they depended on the meager rations they were supplied, and the viciousness of these marauders was legend. Several families lost a young son or an old man to these gangs, even though the victims had never donned a uniform for either side.

But although the mouth of Greasy Creek soon became depopulated as families moved farther up the creek, foragers learned not to venture too far from the river in their searches. Several such parties had been sent scurrying from the place when fusillades of bullets and arrows descended on them, seemingly out of nowhere, as if the mountains themselves had opened up in their wrath. Men may have died on several such occasions, although no one professed to have seen anything, and if any bodies were produced by these skirmishes, they were not recovered. Elisha's black-haired friends could melt into the trees like phantoms and any bloody cargoes they accumulated would disappear into the thick forest cover without a trace.

Greasy Creek had a reputation for isolationism when I was growing up, due largely, I thought, to the difficulties in getting there across the creaking swinging bridge over the river or the poorly maintained roads, but I know now it began long before I was born. I suspect its unflattering reputation began during the War, when strangers were no longer welcomed and were looked upon with suspicion, usually for good reason. The War had changed Greasy Creek forever, and even after the last regiment had mustered out, life was little improved.

But foragers had learned Greasy Creek's wrath early on, or at least Elisha's, and I suspect there are more graves there than just those in the family plots. More than once, I was told of places we were not to play because there were graves there. I suspect that high up on the mountainsides are forgotten tombs of young men who in their youthful lunacy did not anticipate giving their lives for a chicken or a few ears of corn. I suspect I have sat on their unmarked plots, blithely smoked a King Edward cigar and listened to my dogs chase foxes through the woods, with no thought of whose bones I was trespassing upon or what ghost was scowling at me in the darkness.

The madness had fully descended on all of Pike County by 1863, just as it had across the country, and things that were once considered base and unthinkable became a part of everyday life. This new life was vile and obscene, but it was endured, because there was no other choice.

"Hard times," Rissie said. "Hard, hard times. I don't know how people made it through."

The creeks and hollows no longer offered sanctuary to the families that settled them. Old men were hanged or shot down in their fields for hiding their sons from those who would impress them into service, and by the end of the War some families were entirely bereft of men. Mothers who once had dreams of raising their children in houses built with sawn wood and fine doors and brightly painted shutters learned to chink cracks in their cabin walls with mud to keep out the winter chill.

No more cotton was grown on Joseph Hopkins's farm, at least not commercially, but there was no market for it anyway. Lucinda and her children, like most mountain families, grew only what they could for food, and when they planted the small amount of cottonseed they retained from previous years, it came up stunted for lack of attention. What little they produced was spun up rapidly to make clothes to replace the fine store-bought items that Lucinda once wore so proudly.

Victoria's trousseau, including a bright linen parasol that she had so patiently collected for her married life, was soon distributed among her sisters. She was the oldest, and the three sisters next to her had grown into her size and needed them, as she would not, for with George's departure she was determined never to marry. Her three youngest sisters could also find items in the chest her father had bought for her when he received his payments for the cotton he sent down the river.

It seemed so much longer than the few years that had elapsed from the days when everyone was prosperous and the future seemed so bright.

"Why did George do it, Belle?" Victoria would ask her cousin. "Why did he leave me?"

But Dorcus had no answer, for how could she explain why George would have taken up arms against the man who would have been his father-in-law had the War not intervened? She had asked herself the same questions, and could not reply.

Although Victoria now infrequently crossed the buffalo paths back to Greasy Creek, mostly because there was too much work to do on Shelby Creek, when she did find a moment she would take long walks with Dorcus up and down the creek to the places she had played with her cousins in their youth. One time they stopped at the falls to talk and sat on the big flat rock that children had worn smooth over ages. Victoria looked at the pool and felt an almost overpowering urge to jump in and swim to the bottom, as if she knew the life she now led was all a dream, and the cold water would awaken her from it and she would find George waiting for her when she came back to the surface. But she did not, because she knew George would not be there, and she was afraid she would want to stay on the bottom until the water turned warm and soothing, like a feather bed on a cold night.

Few nights passed when Victoria did not feel that the whippoorwills were singing just to her, although she felt merely what every other young girl who had been left behind felt when they heard the same plaintive song.

Joseph had left some money with Lucy and the girls and Dorcus made them husband what funds they had. She had a harder time keeping Clarinda and her family fed, for their resources were drained much earlier, as Zachariah had been gone longer and their farm was smaller and less fertile than the wider fields of Shelby Creek. Clarinda had two sons, where Lucinda had only one, but the losses of four of her children before the War began had weakened her far more than she realized, both mentally and physically. She had never been without her man working with her, she in her kitchen garden and he in the fields with his mules, and she longed for his touch. Sometimes her children would discover that she had wandered away from her garden to another tiny field that she could see every morning from her cabin door, a field where nothing placed in the earth came back.

She would pluck the weeds from around the stones that Zachariah marked and placed there, all the while talking to them as if they were live children, like the ones who continued to work as their mother drifted away. Passersby stopped speaking to her when they found her staring, wide-eyed, at those small graves, for they knew she had lost the ability to respond. Her family soon became dependent on the kindnesses of those who could spare a little bacon or corn meal or some shuck beans. It was humiliating and hurtful and she still did not have enough to feed her family.

One day she made a conscious decision.

"No more of my babies," she shook her head and said to the stones. "No more of you to die."

She had grimly determined that she would do whatever it took to keep her children alive, no matter what that meant. Anything, anything at all: she would do whatever it took.

"No more to die," Rissie said. "That's what Clary said. She wouldn't lose any more of her babies."

I did not know what my grandmother was talking about when she told me that, and she did not elaborate. Not until twenty years after Rissie died did I learn the implications of what Clarinda said to those stones, and why one day she suddenly asked Dorcus for rouge to cover her sallow cheeks.

Anything, she said, anything at all.

Although no family escaped the destruction of the life they once led, the Confederate families had the worst time of it. Union boys managed to send or bring money home, but neither Joseph nor Zachariah, nor any other Confederate soldier, could help their wives much; the irregular paydays they received were rarely in gold, and Confederate paper was worth nothing in Pike County. Even Elisha had stopped accepting it when he delivered whiskey to Virginia, as he did regularly, and he often took payment in salt or coffee or household items his women needed. Occasionally, he would bring back a bolt of cloth for them, knowing that Dorcus would appropriate some of it for the two prostrate families she now oversaw, but he said nothing.

Money was scarce, and Elisha could have sold his goods for solid Union dollars if he had taken the river north, but he rarely went that way anymore. Eastern Kentucky was fought over by both sides and slipping more into lawlessness every day, and though he had no fear for his own safety, he would not risk the loss of a father to his three families. Although he made much less profit by limiting his business, he somehow felt safer when he crossed the picket lines at Pound Gap to sell his whiskey. At least on the other side of the border, he felt, people were not so divided and angry at each other. The Virginia families whose men joined the Union had already fled, usually to Pike County, and he could feel less tension there, although he knew there was infinitely more sorrow. Lum, the brother in blue, was somewhere patrolling in Kentucky and Elisha longed to see him, but he looked forward to his trips through Pound Gap, where the Southwest Virginia Brigade served, to see the brother he carried from Old Virginia forty years before.

This awful conflict will be over soon, everyone agreed. How could it go on much longer? Elisha was not sure it would end so soon and he did not care who won; he just wanted his family back.

Although the news from the West was almost uniformly bad for the Confederacy, in the East the South was winning and with those successes, it was certain that the North and the South would soon make peace. Word had come that spring of Chancellorsville, and with that victory, everyone knew that peace was just around the corner. No one could beat Robert E. Lee, and the death toll was climbing; surely no one would continue a fight that they could never win. The North simply could not defeat the South, at least in Virginia. Even opposing families began to speak to each other again; the War could not last much longer and things would finally get back to normal.

But in July, word came of Gettysburg, and only one of Clarinda's three brothers who marched off with Zachariah to join the Thirty-fourth Virginia sent word that he was safe. One fell in Pennsylvania and was buried there with dozens of other men in butternut in a mass grave on a hot Fourth of July, but the other was never seen again. Years later, a Pike County family traveling to Oregon sent back a letter to Greasy Creek that they had seen one of the Adkins boys driving horses somewhere in the West, but he said nothing and rode away when they asked him his name. But no one could be sure it was sure it was him, for it had been so many years since they last saw the dark-haired boy who marched away to war with his brothers, and they remembered more his name on the casualty lists than the boy himself.

As the summer of 1863 turned to fall, his name was added to others slowly fading in the sunlight that flooded Hamilton's store on the river at Millard, just above the mouth of Greasy Creek. The lists, both Union and Confederate, were hung on opposite sides of the front door, tacked onto the board-and-batten walls, until they nearly reached the floor: sick, they read; wounded, died in camp, died in battle. Some families eventually placed markers in their family cemeteries for sons or brothers they knew would never come back again. In the spring of 1864, one of the Adkins families placed two markers on empty graves in their family cemetery. One was for young Jesse, who died at the Union Thirty-ninth's camp in Louisa of measles. His brother, Henry D., attended him on his deathbed, along with my great-great-great grandfather, Ezekiel Prater. Winright, another brother to Jesse, heard the news later, at the Confederate Tenth's camp in Saltville, Virginia and took his loss in silence.

Only a few hours before Jesse died, his wife Lucy and their three-year-old daughter Nancy arrived by steamboat from Pikeville. Lucy knew he was dying and had planned to take his body home, but she contracted the disease herself and died a few days later. They buried her beside her husband in the soldier's cemetery at Louisa and the men of the Thirty-ninth took care, as best they could, of the three-year-old girl until the family came from Greasy Creek to retrieve her. The family placed the other marker in the Adkins cemetery for her. A hundred years later, construction for a fast-food restaurant in Louisa destroyed the last traces of their graves.

In spite of the losses at Gettysburg and Vicksburg, the Confederacy went on, and Greasy Creek's women looked toward only another hard, lonesome winter without their men. With most of the boys gone, Elisha turned even more to Dorcus as his confidante. Their relationship had always been more like father and son than father and daughter. He would share things with her that he would not share even with the women who had borne his children. In spite of his three wives, he would always speak first to Dorcus when he returned from trips outside Greasy Creek.

Once, after Elisha had made another delivery across Pine Mountain, Dorcus opened the gate to his compound and came over to him as he and his Cherokees unhitched his mule team from the wagon. As the mules were led away, he pulled Dorcus aside and put his arm on her shoulder.

"They're sending the Tenth down to Tennessee," he nearly whispered. "They been transferred to Longstreet at Knoxville. That's that big general that took Stonewall's place."

Elisha was not happy when he heard of a Southern victory at Chickamauga, although it had nothing to do with supporting one side or the other. How could he? His family was on both sides, and Pike County was right in the middle with bad news coming from east and west. With word of the loss at Gettysburg, there was some hope for peace: that the South would realize it could not win, and that the bloodshed would end. And as if to further underscore the impending disaster to the Confederacy, the flamboyant General John Hunt Morgan had taken the Tenth with him on a raid into Kentucky and gotten captured, further adding to the bad news.

Joseph and Zachariah had made their way back unharmed from the disaster, and were chased by some of their own kinfolk in the Thirty-ninth to Joseph's farm, which was now the main rendezvous point for Confederate troopers coming back from raids into Kentucky. Their eyes revealed what they had seen, but at least for a few hours they were home. Now, with another Confederate victory, the blood was up again and the War would surely be prolonged, and that meant more troops would be taken out of the hills to places even farther from home, places they had never heard of before.

"I don't know where they'll wind up, Belle," he said. "They told me over in Gladesville that Yankee raiders come over there all the time, and if the boys are gone long, the whole God damn place will go up."

"Don't tell the women," he said conspiratorially. "Wait till we hear more."

Dorcus nodded her head, but his words stung her: did he not understand that she was a woman too? True, she had no man, and there might be no man left when the War ended, if it ever would. But she was growing tired of never being allowed to be a woman. When she was growing up she had few beaus, for no one would risk her father's wrath, but she knew that one day she would have all the swains of Greasy Creek at her feet. She would do her father's work for a time, but he would eventually let her find a mate. He would have to: Elizabeth and Bethina, her older sisters, were already married. Elizabeth, impetuous and sprightly, had married at sixteen, just after New Year's in 1853. Bethina married three years later, when she was not yet eighteen. Both sisters had children, and Dorcus loved them like she would love her own, but when would she have her own? In the late fall of 1863, as winter began to creep through the hills, Dorcus was twenty-five years old and still a virgin in spite of her age.

Maybe it was because he named me after Mam, Dorcus thought. Maybe he thought that giving me her name would make me like her. But then he calls me Belle. I ain't Mam, I'm me. Damn him. When's he going to learn that?

For as long as she could remember, she had served as Elisha's mediator, his settler of disputes, his deputy, and she was getting weary of the role and fearful that she would never be anything more. She was the confidante of his wives and daughters, and in spite of her sex, older brother to the boys of his families, playing as roughly with them as Elisha would. Who else could serve that role? George was, well, George was George, a fool in love with Victoria, who would never speak to him again. When he joined the Union, Victoria's heart was only a little more shattered than Elisha's, who wanted his family to have no part of either side, but mercifully he was the last to go.

And now there was no one left but Dorcus, who wanted to be as flirty as Elizabeth was at fifteen, as beautiful as Bethina was at seventeen, and yet wanted also to be the rock that the elder Dorcus was. In her mind that conflict hovered eternally. Damn you, Pap, have you taken my life away from me? Will I be an old woman and never know the love of a man or the love of children? But, as she always did, she said nothing to her father, and waited for him to speak again.

"But listen here," he added, even more secretively. "Joe ain't goin' with them."

Dorcus looked at her father incredulously: surely Joseph would not desert, she thought.

Her father continued: "They got a dozen sick horses over in Gladesville they're sendin' back to Abingdon with the rest of the nags. They're worn-out, shoeless, spavined, starved to death, but they need 'em. I hear they're goin' to drive them back behind the lines, maybe to North Carolina, or maybe Patrick County for the winter, and they're goin' to give 'em to Joe to tend to."

Dorcus's heart leapt at the words her father spoke: "They are? Why would they do that, Pappy?"

"They got to," Elisha replied. "He's the best man with horses they got, and he knows the way back there, and that's about the only place safe for horses or any other God damn thing. But it ain't yet for sure, so don't tell Lucy, and don't speak a word of it to Clary, 'cause Zack won't be goin' with him."

"I won't, Daddy," she said. "I promise." And he turned away from her and headed toward the cabins where his women awaited him. Dorcus watched him as he stopped at her mother's cabin without going in. He had not slept in her house for over two years now, and he rarely stayed at Sally's even though she had presented him with a new son this year. He would probably stay again with Haley, who was pregnant again with their fifth child.

Will he ever stop having children, she wondered?

Within a few weeks, word came to Elisha that indeed the Tenth was dispatched to Longstreet and Joseph was given a few smooth-chinned boys to help him drive the horses into Patrick County, on the North Carolina border, for the winter. He would find a place to keep them and stay with them until the spring, but the men would have to return. Southwest Virginia was dangerously short of men, and everyone was needed at their posts. Joseph would have to rely on Home Guards in Patrick to help him protect the herd, but it was far from the danger of raiding parties and there were still Hopkinses there, kinfolk he could depend on.

Joseph sent word to his brother that when he felt the time was right, he should bring Lucy and the children to him. It would be safer in Patrick County, he said. Starving families would be skulking around what remained of Joseph's farm, waiting for an opportunity to poach the food they had collected during the year, and Elisha should take it for his family. By the first frost, Elisha had moved what valuables Lucy had to his compound and collected her family for the trip. They would set out for Abingdon to board the train to Wytheville and then catch the Danville train south. The family would have Christmas in the place where their father was born. Elisha almost envied them.

All of the children went except Victoria; although she loved her father and longed to see him, she would not leave Dorcus and her duties. At least that was the excuse she gave Elisha as he bundled the family into the wagon for the trip through Pound Gap and loaded a few barrels of whiskey to pay their fare.

"Are you sure, girl?" he asked her. "You won't see them till spring."

"Yes, sir, Uncle Lige," she replied. "Tell Daddy I love him, but I got to stay with Belle. Clary's havin' a right smart of trouble and needs help and Belle can't do it all."

Elisha knew that was not the real reason, although Clarinda indeed had few resources left. With Joseph's family gone, Belle would have more time to help Clarinda, and perhaps the increased attention would dissuade Zachariah's wife from doing what Elisha feared she would do, and maybe already had. In spite of the many children she had borne for Zachariah and in spite of her from lack of food, she was still a handsome woman, and there were some men who had not gone away to war or had come back as deserters and they had money. Elisha knew of Clarinda's vow to lose no more of her children. He also knew that Victoria stayed because she knew of George's disillusionment with the life of a soldier and his attendant desertions, and Elisha knew she was beginning to forgive George for what he did.

Bless their hearts, he thought. Maybe they'll be all right after all. Maybe Joe will stay in Patrick County and this God damn war will be over by spring.

But Elisha did not truly believe it would end before Joseph could come home; his vision had not been proven wrong yet, and in December, he heard that General Morgan had escaped from his Ohio penitentiary and was on his way back to Abingdon to reform his command. That would mean more fighting when the roads dried up in spring, and the Southwest Virginia Brigade would need both Joseph and his horses. Elisha also learned that the Tenth would stay with Longstreet in Tennessee during the winter. He had no choice but to tell Clarinda what he knew. When he tried to give her some money, she refused and instead offered money to him. Without even a smattering of hope that Zachariah would be close enough to take care of her, Clarinda used the last gold she had to buy a cask of Elisha's whiskey.

She had already determined the profit she could make from selling it by the drink, and she knew men would pay more if her white fingers surrounded the cup that was offered them. There was little Elisha could do; he knew he had no right to interfere nor could he offer any example of his own morality to dissuade her. During the winter that followed, more than a few riders passed his compound on their way to Clarinda's cabin and soon Dorcus would come from it with Clarinda's children in tow. Even in the dead of winter, with snow covering the trees, it was not unusual to hear fiddle music all night long as the dim light from her window stayed on until dawn.

Early one morning, Elisha was awakened by his dogs barking at someone at the front gate. He rose from the bed he shared with Haley and looked through the frost-covered window to see a figure fumbling with the latch. He swiftly pulled on his breeches and boots, threw a coat over his shoulders and drew his revolver to go outside and confront the intruder.

"Who are you?" he demanded, as the figure, unsuccessful at working the latch, fell off the gate while attempting to cross it. "What do you want, you son-of-a-bitch?"

Elisha raised his gun and drew a bead on the man who struggled to his feet.

"Whoa, Lige," said the man. "It's just me, your ol' nephew Winright."

"Winright?" asked Elisha. "Winright Adkins?"

"Yeah, it's me," he replied, slurring his words.

"Are you drunk?"

"Uh, just a tad. I had me a little taste or two."

"What the hell are you doing here? I thought you were in Tennessee with the army."

"I had to . . . I had to come home to sell some horses. I got . . . I got some fine ones. You want one?"

"I don't see any horses," said Elisha, lowering his weapon and putting it in his pocket.

"Well, that's just it. I sold 'em all but one, and I thought I hitched him here last night, but he ain't here this mornin'."

By now, Elisha's cabins had all awakened, and Dorcus came out into the cold to see what the commotion was about.

"Is anything wrong, Daddy?" she asked.

"Nah, except your fool cousin Winright's drunk as a skunk. Says he lost his horse."

"He didn't lose it, Daddy. I put it up for him."

"Where'd you put it?"

"I put it in the barn and took off its saddle," she said sheepishly. "It looked pitiful out here in the cold."

"Well, go get it," he ordered. "He's too God damn drunk to saddle it."

"No, sir," Winright interjected. "I can do it. Where's the barn?"

"Shut up and come in the house," Elisha replied, as Dorcus ran up the road to the tiny bridge that crossed the creek to Clarinda's farm. "You're in no shape to saddle a sawhorse."

"By God, I am too," Winright said as he drunkenly staggered toward the path Dorcus had taken. Elisha grabbed his arm to restrain him.

"I said get in the God damn house!"

Winright opened his eyes widely, shook his head, and allowed himself to be led into the compound. Even as inebriated as he was, he knew not to challenge Elisha Hopkins.

"Yeah, I made me a little money," he said, as Elisha pulled him through the door of the Haley's cabin. "'Course I just spent most of it, but it was worth every God damn cent." In spite of her condition, Haley rose from her bed and lit a fire on the hearth when Elisha went outside. Seeing the fire, Winright slumped against the chimney, his head banging painfully against the mantle as he stretched his hands out to warm them.

Elisha asked him again: "I thought you boys were in Tennessee. How'd you get a pass?"

"No pass," Winright burbled. "I just had to sell my horses. Hell, I was up in the valley when the boys pulled out for Tennessee. They put me guardin' the saltworks. Ain't nobody goin' to miss me. I'll tell 'em sumpin' when I get back."

"Well, you'd better get your ribey ass back there soon," Elisha warned him.

Haley hung a blackened pot over the fire after pouring in water and some of the precious coffee they still had. It had begun to boil by the time Dorcus arrived with Winright's horse.

"I got his horse, Daddy," she said as she opened the door and came inside.

"Go on back to the house, Belle," he told her. "I'll take care of this." Elisha ignored the deadly stare she cast at Winright.

After the coffee was ready, Winright and Elisha sat at the table as Winright drank.

"You ain't got nothing stronger I can put in it this, do you?" Winright asked.

"No, by God, and you don't need it," Elisha replied. "Now listen here you God damn fool: You got no pass. You probably stole those horses, and if a Yankee patrol catches you, your ass is gone. You drink that up and get on your horse and go see your family. And then you get out of Greasy Creek before you get caught."

"Now, Lige . . . " Winright began.

"Don't 'Now Lige' me, boy!" Elisha demanded. "I'm tellin' you: Get on that horse and get gone."

Reasonably sober now, Winright did as he was ordered and rose to his feet. He shook hands with Elisha as he went out the door. As he mounted his horse, Elisha walked over to the gate and opened it. "You heard what I told you?" Elisha asked.

"Yep, I heard," he said as he rode through. "I'll do it. Be seein' you, Lige."

Elisha, shaking his head, watched him fade into the mist rising up from the creek. When Elisha turned around, Dorcus was beside him again.

"I don't like that man, Daddy," she said.

"Well, he's your kinfolk," Elisha replied. "Sometimes you got to take the good with the bad." And he laughed: "Sometimes, they can be pretty bad."

"You know he stayed with Clary all night, don't you?" she asked him.

"Ain't none of our business, girl," Elisha said. "Ain't nothin' I can do. Now you get on back in the house. It's cold this mornin'."

"I still don't like him," she said as she turned to go back to the cabin she shared with her mother, where Clarinda and Zachariah's children were sleeping. She would let them sleep for a while longer before she awakened them and took them back to their mother. They would not see their father again until spring, but Winright would come back, and others, and by the time the redbuds bloomed again on Greasy Creek, the children had become familiar with their mother's visitors.

During the rest of the winter, far away from Greasy Creek, Lucinda and her children, all except Victoria, lived with Joseph, almost on the farm where he was born in Patrick County, the place where the pioneer Hopkinses, Thackers, and Adkinses of Pike County all came from. A note on Joseph's service record lists him as being "paid for tending horses for four months." It was for December, January, February and March. For at least one Christmas during the War, at least part of the Hopkins family was almost united and as happy as any family could have been in those dark years.

When the family returned to Shelby Creek, Victoria and Dorcus had Lucinda's garden planted. A lettuce bed was turning light green, dark green onions were beginning to thrust out of the soil, and pea vines were already climbing poles when Joseph's family tumbled out of Elisha's wagon. Elisha had already plowed the ground for potatoes, and a great pile of fish from the river was rotting happily into fertilizer in wooden tubs near the chicken coop. He had also brought over a half-dozen setting hens that had already assumed control of the barnyard and indignantly clucked at the children as they approached. It was not much more than Joseph and Lucinda had when they first set up housekeeping, but it would have been a perfect homecoming for the family had their father been with them.

During the winter, Victoria had seen George once, but did not tell her mother of his visit. He had somehow acquired a legitimate pass to come home, but Elisha still ordered him to stay alone at the cabin on Ripley Knob. It was still too dangerous to walk around in any uniform in Pike County, and on a cold and snowy day, Phoebe allowed Victoria and Dorcus to take food to the refugee. In spite of his father's admonition to tough it out in the cold until dark, he lit the fire early for their visit, and Dorcus scolded him when they arrived.

"How long you had this going, George?" she asked, when they walked into the warm cabin. "You know very well people could see the smoke before dark."

"It'll be all right, Sister," he replied. "I just didn't want you to be cold when you all got here."

But if Victoria had not come with her, he would not have taken the chance, and Victoria was flattered by his act, although she remained wary with him and did not speak to him immediately. George attempted to greet Victoria, but found that his mouth had become so dry and his tongue so thick that he was unable to say a word.

"Well, sit down and eat," said Dorcus. "It's fixin' to snow, and we'd better get gone before it gets too bad to walk home."

George obediently sat down in one of the rough chairs Elisha and Joseph had painstakingly put together years before when they built the cabin. It was intended to be a showplace for the boys, a way of demonstrating to their father that they were now men and capable of doing the work required of men, and they had split and planed logs to make a floor when most of the cabins on Greasy Creek had dirt floors. The table, two chairs, and a rope bed was all the furniture the cabin could boast, although Elisha had put in a windowpane with glass when he brought his first bride there thirty years before. On some nights, Elisha would still leave the compound and his three wives to go up Ripley Knob to build a great fire in front of the cabin and drink with his Indian friends until daylight. He always found it the way he left it; the Indians watched over it for Elisha when no one was there.

As George ate and Dorcus peered nervously through the window, watching for approaching riders, Victoria stared at the fire George had prepared for her. All three of them struggled to find something to say, common ground for discourse, words that would not remind them of the War and its losses, but that was impossible. Everything had been affected by the War and there was nothing that would not lead a casual conversation back into politics. None of the three young people in that cabin that night could formulate any thought that they could utter without worry as to its reception. George was the lucky one; he was excused from his obligation to speak as long as he was eating. Victoria could speak little with her heart bursting out of her chest, so again it fell to Dorcus to begin the conversation.

"Daddy sent you some whiskey to keep you warm," she said, producing a bottle she had hidden under her coat. "But he said not to drink it all up at one time. Everything's getting' scarce."

"I won't," George said thankfully. "I'll take care of it."

At one time in his life, George would never have let Victoria think he would touch a drop, but the time for pretense had passed and they all knew it. He took the bottle and placed it in his saddlebag.

"Daddy said the Indians will bring your horse back to you in the morning," she continued. "He said to take the high trails out of Pike County. There are too many bushwhackers on the main roads."

George merely nodded his head when Dorcus spoke. Elisha had told him the same thing earlier in the day.

Dorcus looked at Victoria, who was staring at the fire and spoke again: "I'm goin' outside to see what the weather's doin'. I could smell snow in the air as we come up the hill."

She looked again at Victoria and George, neither of whom was looking at her or each other. It was time for her to give them a moment alone and she opened the door and walked outside. After a long pause, the lovers finally acknowledged each other.

"I heard . . . I heard your family went out to the old place for the winter," George awkwardly spoke. "I went out there once with Pappy and it's a right pretty place. Big ol' mountains and then flat land all the way to the ocean. I once seen that, too."

"They say it is," Victoria finally spoke. "I never been there."

"It's . . . It's a right pretty place," he repeated himself.

"That's what they say," she repeated herself.

"I guess I'm goin' back tomorrow," George said.

"Un-huh," she said, forcing herself to make some reply, but knowing neither what to say nor how to say it.

"Victoria, I hope you can . . . I mean . . . I hope you understand . . . That is . . . I . . ."

"I understand, George," she finally said, releasing him from his agony. "I mean, I guess I understand. They say bushwhackers are killing people and stealing everything they get their hands on."

"I know, I know," he said frantically, as if he had just been offered some absolution from his sins. "That's the only reason I joined up. I was afraid nobody could help us besides the government troops."

"I spent most of my time chasing bushwhackers," he continued. "They ain't for the North or the South. They're all rogues. They don't believe in nothin'."

"But what will you do if you ever meet Daddy?" she asked him.

"Nothin', I swear. If we ever run into Uncle Joe, I swear I'll desert."

"They can shoot you for that, Belle says," Victoria replied.

"I know that, but I couldn't take a chance on . . ." George started to say, "killing," but bit his tongue. "You know what I mean."

"You know that Daddy wouldn't have any choice if he met you or Lum or Andrew or any of the boys who went over to the other side?" In Victoria's mind, as well as Dorcus', the South was the only side. "You know that, don't you?"

"That's why I won't take a chance. I ain't gonna fight your daddy."

She finally looked square George in the eyes. "You promise?" she asked.

"I promise," said George as he walked toward her. He had walked toward her and had almost touched the hands she had raised to meet him when Dorcus opened the door and abruptly re-entered the cabin. She saw George and Victoria backlit by the fireplace and only inches separating them and smiled to herself, knowing that her short hiatus had achieved some good results.

"It's snowin' out there," she said, brushing off a few snowflakes. "Time for us to go, Sister."

The lovers forced back the momentum that had propelled them toward each other, but George recaptured it and took Victoria's hand in his. Years later, Dorcus would tell the story that it may have been merely sparks popping out of the fire, but she saw something travel between George and Victoria that night, a blue-white light that arced between them, as she picked up the pan George had emptied in his hunger.

"You take this cornbread and bacon for your trip," she said as she puttered about the table. "Good-bye, Brother."

She pecked him on the cheek and turned to go outside, leaving George and Victoria to say their good-byes. George did not acknowledge her departure.

When Victoria came back out and took Dorcus's hand for the treacherous walk back down the mountain in the snow, Dorcus could see her flushed face even without a moon. They could barely see in front of them, but they knew the path well. When they reached the bottom of the hill, Dorcus asked the question that she wanted to ask since they left the mountaintop.

"Did you kiss him?" she asked, as Victoria giddily danced through the snow on the now level ground, but she did not reply.

"Victoria?" she asked again. "Did you kiss my brother good-bye?"

"Yes, Belle, I did," Victoria finally replied. "Is that bad?"

"No," said Dorcus. "There ain't nothin' bad about it. You love him; he loves you. Ain't no war, ain't no army, Yankee or Confederate, ain't nothin' goin' to change that."

"You remember that as long as you live," she added, but it was unnecessary, for Victoria had fallen in love with George all over again and as they walked into the night, the cousins once more began making plans for the wedding.

Here Be Dragons

*I*t wasn't the first time I had spoken to the Sons of Confederate Veterans, but I had new information this time and I said nothing as I waited through the rituals and the business session and other speakers. It was a small group, but well-informed, and I did not have to make many of the explanations I did to other groups. During the previous year, I had written newspaper columns on the Civil War in Eastern Kentucky, and with the recently emerging interest in the War, I often received invitations to speak to different groups. Some of my audiences were surprised to find the tragedy of the Civil War did not exclude our people, since most of them were no better schooled in our history than I was before I began my search. Like me, their interest developed in spite of the lack of classroom lessons, rather than because of them. But now I had published my first book and I was going to share with them some of what I had written.

My topic was the first Battle of Saltville, largely ignored in most Civil War history books, but listed as being fought on October 2, 1864, when it was even mentioned. I had been asked to speak about the battle, the greatest battle ever fought between Eastern Kentuckians, although it was not fought in Eastern Kentucky, but across the state line in Saltville, Virginia. It is an easy two-hour drive from Pikeville today, but in 1864 it took the 5200-man army of Union General Stephen Gano Burbridge the better part of a week to make the trip after they drove Confederate pickets away from the Big Sandy town and occupied it on September 27.

When I mentioned Burbridge's name, the expected groan went up from the SCV boys, for Burbridge, who died mostly forgotten in Brooklyn, New York in 1894, is still the most hated man in Kentucky *history, especially by SCV members. A capable general and military commander of Kentucky, Burbridge was ostracized in his native state for his infamous General Order 59, his attempt to quell the rising tide of guerrilla activity that plagued Kentucky when he took command. His order said that he would pull four Confederate prisoners out of prison camps and summarily execute them for any Union soldier bushwhacked. He later extended the order to any killing of Negroes in Kentucky. His ploy was unsuccessful, and even Kentucky Unionists ultimately petitioned Abraham Lincoln to remove him from office because of public revulsion to the Order and its application. If anything, it had the opposite effect of what Burbridge intended; it hardened Confederate resolve and engendered sympathy for the victims. By February of 1865, Lincoln had replaced Burbridge, but when the general led his army through Pikeville to the saltworks, he was still at the height of his powers and he used them fearfully.*

Although my presentation was on the battle itself, General Order 59 always came up in any discussion of Burbridge. As a result of the order, at least fifty regular Confederate soldiers, none of whom had anything to do with the killings they paid for with their lives, were shot in full view of crowds Burbridge ordered out from nearby towns and villages. Their bullet-torn bodies were then left on the field for local residents to attend to. Union troops were forbidden to bury the unarmed men they had just killed. By the time the carnage ended, even the firing squads were beginning to resist their orders.

The first part of my presentation was on the battle, and I spoke of the skirmishes in Pikeville and how Burbridge took the old Virginia Turnpike, the Grundy road, out of Pikeville in an attempt to envelop Saltville in a pincer movement from the north. Another Federal army, led by General Alvan Gillem, was to approach from the south, out of Knoxville, Tennessee, and together they would crush the saltworks with overwhelming force. The plan was to cut off the flow of vitally needed salt, since Saltville was supplying the needs of nearly the entire South east of the Mississippi River. Without salt, there would be no way to preserve food for the coming winter and the armies and the people of the Confederacy would be starved into submission.

It was a good plan and had been hatched the year before in a hotel room in Louisville when Ulysses S. Grant met with William T.

Sherman and planned the South's defeat. This was Burbridge's part of the Grand Design and his chance at glory. It was also the second trip to Saltville for the hated general, having had to abort his previous mission during the summer when he received word that General John Hunt Morgan was advancing west into the Bluegrass as he was heading east. He turned around and smashed Morgan's army at Cynthiana, but had to wait and refit his troops before he could again advance on Saltville.

Burbridge had great confidence, but he did not know that General Gillem had been called back by an overly cautious General Ambrose Burnside in Tennessee, who was still smarting from his defeat at the head of the Union Army in the Battle of Fredericksburg two years before. But even with the loss of the entire southern vanguard of the pincer movement, Burbridge's 5200 well-fed and well-supplied troopers outnumbered the less than 700 half-clothed and hungry defenders of the saltworks. I reminded my audience of the warnings the old cartographers applied to uncharted waters. They would write "Here Be Monsters" or "Here Be Dragons" on the edge of their maps. But the Southwest Virginia troops could not have known the great huffing, snorting, terrible thing was coiling through the hills toward them.

I took my audience on a verbal excursion from Pikeville to Cedar Bluff, just outside Richlands, where the Confederate Tenth Kentucky Cavalry established its first redoubt. Most of my audience descended from soldiers in the Tenth, although many, like me, also had ancestors in the Union Thirty-ninth Kentucky. Still, it was hard not to sympathize with the Confederate boys. With less than 150 cavalrymen remaining, the Tenth was a shell, albeit a hard shell, of the great regiment Jack May had created over two years before, and they knew the odds were against them in the coming fight.

But neither the Thirty-ninth nor any of the Union Army, which included two new regiments of black soldiers, had an easy go of it. Harassed by snipers, victim to the treacherous roads and passes of the Levisa Fork, and exhausted from the forced march from Pikeville, Burbridge's army was hungry and footsore when it mounted its first action against entrenched Confederate forces at Cedar Bluff. Lt. Colonel Edwin Trimble, who had taken over the Tenth after Jack May resigned, arrayed his troops on the narrow pass above the town in an attempt to use the geography of the region against the intruder. Trimble knew his orders were suicidal and his men were expendable, but he would use them wisely as the sheer volume of soldiers pushed him back from position to position, until Burbridge finally rested his men on the night of October 1, just upriver from the saltworks.

The next day, Burbridge faced 2800 Confederates on the ridges outside Saltville, and could not budge them in spite of repeated charges. After night fell, he had his men build bonfires to convince his enemy that his men were merely resting until morning and slipped away under cover of darkness. The expedition was a defeat, but his withdrawal was skillful and he returned to Lexington with most of his army intact. Saltville held on for two more months, until December, when it fell during Christmas to an overwhelming force of Union firepower.

My audience grumbled some more about Burbridge after I finished my presentation, but agreed that he was a skilled general in spite of the personal hatred they all felt for the man. One had to give the devil his due. But then I announced that I had some new information on General Order 59 and the muttering ceased. I passed around copies of documents I had recently acquired from the National Archives and an accompanying letter from the archivist.

"These are execution orders of a Pike County boy, another one of Burbridge's victims," I said. "I thought you'd like to see them."

I could almost hear their hearts beating. A Pike County boy? Until I received the documents, the only known Eastern Kentucky victim of Burbridge's atrocities was a soldier named John May Hamilton, from Johnson County, on down the Big Sandy. As I passed out the copies and the accompanying letter, I explained how I had gotten them and why the archivist could not find a report on the execution, even though the orders, in usual military fashion, required a report to be submitted.

"The reason was, Burbridge verbally ordered no reports to be made," I said. "In this case, eight men were on the orders, but only three were shot. Burbridge had the men choose who would die by drawing beans out of a hat: eight beans, five white and three red. Those who drew the red beans were dead men."

I could feel the heat rise in my audience, as they had now learned of someone from Pike County who had fallen to Burbridge's wrath.

"This was a violation of military protocol," I continued. "But that was typical of his administration and that's part of the reason Lincoln canned him."

"Why did he make them draw on who would die?" one of the SCV members asked.

"He thought that would further demoralize the Confederates," I explained. "He wanted the entire state to act against bushwhackers and guerrillas and thought if the Confederate POW's had a hand in killing other POW's then the movement would cease. Of course, it didn't work; the Unionists were the ones becoming demoralized because of Burbridge's excesses."

The new rage of the SCV members was palpable. "Where's that son-of-a-bitch buried?" one of the men asked me. "I'd like to take a leak on his grave."

"Me, too," another said.

"Unfortunately, he's buried at Arlington," I said, and that was all that was necessary to quell the idea. Arlington is sacred soil to all Americans, and to SCV members it was even more so because it was Lee's home first, before it became the final resting place of the bravest of America's brave. My audience felt that Burbridge had no business resting in that hallowed place, and I agreed.

Before the meeting ended, the men carefully folded the copies I had made for them and tucked them away safely. I could see the reverence they felt, not for the hateful pages, but for the names on them. Some of the men said they were going to frame their copies and hang them on their walls, to remind them of a Pike County boy, another victim and hero they had not known before that night.

But I was told of him long before, although I did not realize it at the time, and I needed the documentation only to prove my story to any skeptics who might not believe me. Of course, I had once been one myself until I learned not to doubt my grandmother's stories.

Indeed I had known him well, even though he died nearly eighty years before I was born. Rissie made sure that I would.

That's why I knew there were dragons.

Chapter Five

Spartans

Dorcus loaded her apron with chop to feed the chickens clucking expectantly inside the coop. Two of the pullets had flown over the fence and were trotting back and forth in front of the gate, anticipating dinner, as she took down a rusty set of shears from the wall of the henhouse and slipped them inside her apron string. Can't afford to lose any more chickens, she thought. Meat and eggs are too precious now and this is all we have left. Oh, to have my geese back.

Dorcus remembered the great hissing gaggles that once dominated the farm, strolling fearlessly among the cabins and barns like emperors. But they had gone long ago, from everyone's farms, and families were blessed just to have chickens. She began tossing handfuls of the ground corn through the rails and after she emptied her apron, she caught each of the wayward pullets in turn, deftly clipped each of their wing feathers and tossed them into the pen. As the last one flopped gracelessly to the ground, she turned to see one of the Indian boys ride wildly up to the front gate and jump from his horse, barely tying it to the fence in his haste. He leaped across the rails and ran into the blacksmith shop where Elisha was pumping the bellows at his forge, preparing to heat iron for horseshoes. "Lisha, Lisha!" she could hear him shout as he disappeared inside.

Oh Lord, she thought, is this what he's been waiting for?

In a moment, Elisha walked hastily to the barn with the boy, and as pulled his saddle off the stall rail and collected his blanket and saddlebag, the boy ran with a bridle to the lot where Elisha's horse stood in anticipation. He barely had time to put the bridle on as the horse snorted its impatience. In a moment, it was saddled and Elisha rode over to her while the Indian boy waited at the gate.

"Army comin' through, Belle," he said. "I 'spect they're goin' to Virginny, but there still might be foragers. Run the hogs up the holler and tell Paw to get his gun and come down here until I get back. Take the mare and foal up to Ripley Knob. I'll be back by daybreak."

"Yes, sir," she said. "You want me to get Uncle John?"

"I'll get him myself," he answered. "Keep the children inside and put out the fires. Don't light any lamps when it gets dark. You got that, girl?"

"Yes, sir."

"They ought to know better than to come up here, but I'm goin' to get the men ready just in case. Paw'll know what to do if they come afore I get back."

He checked his revolver and felt for additional cartridges in the pocket of his coat. "Tell Haley . . . Tell the women not to worry," he said and rode through the gate, barely pausing for the Indian boy to close it and mount his own horse to ride after him.

This is it, she thought, this is really it. Sweet Jesus, Lord, please keep all of them safe.

She ran from cabin to cabin, telling the women and children what Elisha had said and then removed the rails from the hog pen to drive the squealing animals up the hollow beyond Cornelius's cabin. She stopped long enough to tell her grandfather what Elisha wanted him to do and by the time she returned, the old man and woman had already left to take their places in defense of the farm.

She then went to the barn and saddled the mare, but she left the foal behind as it protested its mother's absence. She had plenty of time to take the animals up to Ripley Knob when she returned, but she had another job to do even if her father had not told her to do it. She had to ride to Shelby Creek to find Victoria.

That was easy enough, George thought, as he listened to the exhausted column pass by him on the narrow mountain trail. The night was pitch-black, and even the starlight was obscured by the clouds that had moved in before dark. When the call went out for outriders to defend the flanks of the army as it moved through enemy territory,

George rode away with the few men who would take the chance of moving alone through the wilderness of the Levisa, and to his relief, the sergeant had not written down who he had assigned the tasks.

During the day, George had ridden up and down the line, diving into the woods when shooting erupted to scatter the hidden Confederates who fired on the column. Before long, he himself had forgotten his position. Most of the torches that had been lit to direct the column through dangerous bends had been extinguished and the men were moving forward in darkness.

When he felt it was safe, he took out the civilian raincoat he had purchased a few days before and put it on. There was still the chance he would be shot by Confederates before he made it home, or discovered by other Federal outriders, but it was a chance he was willing to take. He turned his horse away from the army that was moving toward Saltville and his Uncle Joe and Zachariah, and quietly began his journey back to Ripley Knob. He'd had enough of soldiering. He was going home.

"Smoked Yankees! Smoked Yankees!" Zachariah yelled maniacally as he waved his hat and stormed toward the small group of horsemen who were awaiting him. Joseph, standing by his horse as his wild-eyed friend neared, had to steady her amid the racket Zachariah made as he approached. Joseph had never seen him so excited.

It was a different Zachariah this morning from the man who sat beside him last night poking the fire morosely as they sat beside the campfire and waited for the scouts to come back from their day's work.

Joseph knew what was troubling his friend, but said nothing. It had never been the same since Zachariah told him the news: "Clary's had a girl," he said. "She named her Adelaide." Joseph understood what he meant when he said "she named her," not "we named her," as a proud father would have said. He had heard the rumors of what Clarinda was doing so that her family would be fed, and that her cousin Winright Adkins was the father of Zachariah's latest child. Joseph had seen the hatred in Zachariah's eyes when he saw him looking at Winright, saw them avoiding each other in camp, as if they both knew what could happen if words were spoken openly about it.

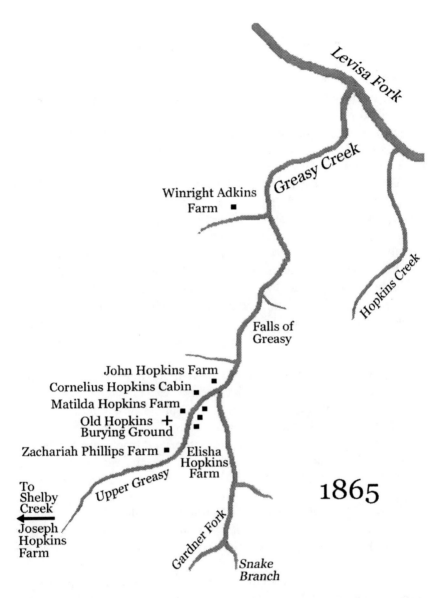

By 1865 Liberty has disappeared and the Cornelius Hopkins homestead is abandoned. The Old Hopkins Burying Ground is across the creek from Elisha Hopkins' farm. Cornelius and Dorcus are living in the cabin their children built for them to protect them from predations along the river. When they die, the new cemetery will be started, as the old cemetery has filled up.

"It's tryin' to rain," Joseph said to Zachariah as he tossed a few more twigs on the fire. "Better cover up the lightwood before it gets wet or we'll have a devil of a time getting' a fire started tomorrow." As he spoke, he noticed a figure moving out of the mist toward him. It was Lt. Colonel Edwin Trimble, the new commander of the Tenth Kentucky. Although younger than Joseph and younger than many other men in his command for that matter, Trimble had performed admirably when given the job after Jack May quit.

That had been a blow to the boys, and many of them began to wonder why they should stay if Jack May no longer had heart in the fight. But Trimble rallied them with his example of bravery and leadership and he had the approval of Joseph, whose success at rescuing the castoff horses the previous year had put many of the Tenth's cavalrymen back in the saddle. Trimble appreciated his work. "Nobody knows a horse like Joseph Hopkins," he said. Twice he had offered Joseph officer's rank and twice Joseph had declined. He told the young commander that he would fight to the death if need be, but would not accept the responsibility of sending other men to their deaths.

The men started to rise when Trimble appeared. "Stay still, gentlemen," he said. "Joseph, will you come with me?"

Out of earshot of the rest of the men, Trimble gave him the news.

"Our pickets skirmished with a large Union force in Pikeville yesterday," he said. "It appears several thousand troops are coming up the Levisa. I have no doubt they are marching on the saltworks."

Joseph was shocked. Several thousand? Against what we have here?

"Joseph, you will put out pickets at Richlands tomorrow and be ready to fall back to Cedar Bluff. We should be able to slow them considerably at the gap there. If they breach our defenses, we will retire to Clinch Mountain."

Joseph nodded his head and Trimble continued: "We cannot fight them on even ground, but we will join the rest of the brigade on the mountain and we should hold there. General Breckinridge is up in the Valley, but is hastening his return with reinforcements."

Joseph wondered where the new troops would come from. Most of the Virginia boys were gone, some serving under Lee, some never to return. It was mostly Kentuckians in the Southwest Virginia Brigade and mostly Kentuckians, he expected, coming toward them. He wondered if he would see Lum across the battle line tomorrow and what he would do if he did.

"I have great faith in you Joseph," Trimble said. "You and your men have done a remarkable job."

Part of Trimble's praise was due to the mere fact that Joseph and his people were still there; sickness and desertions, mostly the latter, had taken a fearful toll on the once-proud regiment. Fewer than 150 men remained.

"Well, sir," Joseph said bravely, as much for his own benefit as the colonel's, "if they want our salt, they'll have to pay for it."

Trimble left to brief the rest of the men and Joseph walked over to his saddlebags to retrieve a bottle his brother had given him. "What'd the colonel say, Joe?" one of the men asked him, but Joseph said nothing until he passed around the bottle while delivering their death warrants. It served its purpose, but Joseph was surprised that Zachariah drank little as the bottle went from man to man. Instead, the dark cloud that seemed to hover over his friend disappeared, and Joseph noted a strange smile on Zachariah's face as he began cleaning his weapons.

"I want to make sure I'm ready for tomorrow's little soirée," he said with a grin.

Before daylight the next morning, the regiment was on the field at Richlands, where Zachariah demanded to be the scout sent closest to the enemy lines. Now he would have the opportunity to use the weapons he had painstakingly cleaned the night before.

As the dust settled, Zachariah gave his report. He could not mask his glee.

"What's the matter with you, boy?" Joseph asked. "You see some yankees or something?"

"All over the God damn place, Joe!" Zachariah replied, grinning demonically. "Shit fire, boy; they're pourin' through the gap like hornets out of a nest. Thousands of 'em. Nigger soldiers too, suckin' up the light."

"Did you see any artillery?" Trimble asked.

"Couldn't tell, sir," said Zachariah formally. "Couldn't even see the end of the column. I never seen so many Yanks."

Other horsemen approached with their reports, confirming what Zachariah had just given, and Trimble mounted his horse, giving commands.

"Private Phillips, pull in our pickets and fall back to the other side of the river at Cedar Bluff," he ordered. "Joseph, get your men situated at the positions we selected. Use good cover and wait for my command to fire."

"Yes, sir!" both men answered as the colonel rode off to align his men for the fracas that would soon come. Joseph mounted his horse and spoke again to Zachariah before riding away.

"Watch yourself out there, you redheaded peckerwood. Just get those boys back in and don't take any chances."

"Aye, I'll watch myself, but if I get a good shot I'll by God take it," Zachariah replied as he turned to ride away. He was still grinning madly at his friend.

"It's comin', Joe," he said. "It's goin' to be a big one. Hah! We're all goin' to die!"

"Just get the boys in!" Joseph shouted to his wild friend. "Watch your skinny ass out there."

"It's comin'," Zachariah shouted back to him. "See you in hell, Joe!"

"Yeah," Joseph said, mostly to himself. "See you in hell, Zack. We'll all be there."

So far, so good, George thought as the horse walked at its own speed up the mountain path. He did not try to rush and stopped occasionally, allowing the horse to graze when they found grassy fields. He was not sure if there would be any grain at the cabin and did not want the horse to neigh in hunger after he got there. He would have to find forage when he got to Ripley Knob, but he had money, if there was any to buy. His first job was to escape the outriders and renegades and make it home. His second job would be to convince Elisha to let him stay.

That would be the hard part. He was more afraid of his father's wrath than the bullets of the enemy, although these days he was not completely sure who that was.

Joseph wheeled his horse around and headed back to the now-abandoned village of Cedar Bluff beside the Clinch River, where the rest of the Tenth was waiting. After assigning three troopers to take the horses back through the pass between the high rock walls behind the town, he assigned several positions to his troops.

"Get under cover and stay down!" he ordered them. "Don't fire until you hear the rest of the line firin'. Don't give away your position."

After a few minutes, the men were in place, but firing had already erupted as the pickets rushed back to safety. Zachariah was the last to arrive.

"That all of 'em?" Joseph asked as Zachariah broke through the dust the other horsemen had created.

"God damn, there's a slew of those sorry bastards out there," he said. "Yeah, all the boys are in."

"Good, get off your horse and follow me." Joseph ordered one of the men to collect the horses and take them through the pass and the rest of the men began climbing the steep canyon walls with him. Bullets were already beginning to whiz through the trees.

"How long we goin' to try to hold here?" Zachariah asked him as they settled into position.

"Until we're relieved or we kill all these sons-of-bitches," Joseph replied.

"Hey, Joe," Zachariah said. "The Thirty-ninth's with that sorry gang, you know."

Joseph knew; he hoped it would not come to it, but his brother and his nephew and so many of what used to be his friends could be coming into his sights at any time, and he would have no choice but to fire. It was the path each of them had chosen, it was their choice, and now they would collide. The War had finally turned personal.

Indeed, Columbus and George were soldiers with the Thirty-ninth, but Joseph did not know that Columbus was sick and the regiment had left him behind in the hospital when it pulled out. Nor did he know that George had deserted again, or that the Federal Army was nearly exhausted from its march.

Their commander knew that, but Burbridge also knew that the sooner he got to Saltville, the fewer troops he would have to face when he got there. He had sent out riders to connect with the other column that was supposed to have struck out from Knoxville at the same time he entered the mountains of Eastern Kentucky, but they had returned empty-handed. Gillem had not arrived and Burbridge began to doubt he would come at all. He had gone this far, however, and he would not turn back. He wanted more than anything to lead a great army out of Kentucky to flay the Rebels on their home soil. Glory was his destiny and nothing on God's earth would prevent him from fulfilling it.

Burbridge and his staff dismounted when they reached a small point on the side of the ridge east of Richlands. Through his field glasses, he watched his troops press toward Cedar Bluff. He could see the Confederates getting into position above the river.

"Captain," he said to his aide as he lowered his glasses. "Do not allow the men to go into the town, but place a heavy fire on it. Keep up a demonstration, but I want men to scale those heights while we keep the Rebels busy. Your objective will be those outcroppings there and this point over here." He pointed to positions that easily overlooked the village and the river, which was now just ankle deep because of the usual fall drought. "Wait until the men are in position and open fire on my command. Quickly, now!"

In a few minutes, Burbridge's troops were inching their way up the rocky walls of the canyon. Smoke was already filling up the tiny valley and obscuring visibility. In spite of both his and Trimble's orders, nervous troops had already begun firing, and both lines now erupted in response.

Trimble peered through his own field glasses at the fighting and spotted the Union commander above the town. He could tell something was wrong; even though the Yankee muskets were peppering his lines, he saw no real forward movement from the other side. He scanned the left hillside above his men, where there was less cover, and could see a slight movement far beyond where his line ended. They're trying to flank us, he thought. He could not see any movement on the right, but sensed that Union troops were moving under the trees there as well.

"Damn!" he muttered to his tiny staff. "Lieutenant, get word to Corporal Hopkins to move his men out of position and fall back through the gap. I fear we are about to be flanked." The young officer immediately ran toward the lines, keeping down to dodge the stream of Union bullets. Just as his men were moving out of their positions, a burst of fire rained down from the high points on either side of the valley.

Joseph and his troops steadily emptied their cartridge cases to cover the other men who were scurrying back to safety and were the last to give up their positions.

"Were any of the men wounded?" Trimble asked Joseph as he arrived at Trimble's location.

"No, sir" Joseph said. "Some of the boys got a little scratched up gettin' out of there, but they're all safe."

"Very good," Trimble replied. "Mount up and let's get through the pass."

Trimble inspected his force at the same intersection that controls traffic today, where the road to Pikeville still connects to the road up to Jeffersonville, now known as Tazewell, and down to Lebanon, which still keeps its ancient name. Across the ridge in front of the intersection is Thompson Valley, where bluebirds still rise in great waves in summer, like the ghosts of Union soldiers who died there nearly a century and a half ago.

But on that late September day in 1864, no one had died yet, and Trimble found his men in high spirits, laughing and joking about the skirmish they had just fought.

"Which way do you think they'll go, Joe?" Zachariah asked as they waited for the troops to assemble. "Up or down?"

"Hell, they got enough men to go both ways," Joseph replied. "That's probably what they'll do." Within a few minutes, Trimble ordered his entire troop south, to the largest of the gaps.

"Joseph," he said, riding up to him. "I suspect General Burbridge will split his force when he arrives here. We need to get back to Colonel Giltner at Liberty Hill. Burbridge may make camp before he comes on, but I doubt it. We have little choice now but to form a redoubt on Clinch Mountain. When all your men clear the gap, take them directly there and locate positions above the Bowen farm. Watch for the other boys; I don't want the brigade cut off in the darkness."

"Yes, sir!" Joseph replied with a salute. Trimble and the rest of the column rode off for Liberty Hill, at the other end of Thompson Valley, as Joseph and his men dashed for the Saltville road. The light had nearly gone as he reached his objective and set his men on the roadbed looking down at a pristine white farmhouse that seemed to shimmer ghostly pale as the stars began to peek through the clouds. Within an hour, the valley was plunged almost into darkness and the men nervously turned toward any sound that echoed through the violet sea that now swelled to the ridges.

In progressively smaller groups, the Southwest Virginia Brigade stormed up the mountain, until the last of them dismounted and took cover. In the distance, the sound of more gunfire could be heard sporadically, along with the sound of horses' hooves and men shouting. Rumors passed up and down the line as the men waited for Burbridge's army to come out of the darkness.

"Hey Joe, you think those bastards'll hit us tonight?" Zachariah asked as he tumbled into place beside his friend and passed a small piece of cheese to him.

"Where'd you get this?" Joseph inquired, taking a bite.

"Found it in a smokehouse in Cedar Bluff," Zachariah replied. "Hell, the Yankees would've taken it anyway and it weren't nobody home. Found me an egg, too, but I done sucked it." He laughed. "It wouldn't have made the trip, and we can't light no fire tonight anyway."

Joseph looked back at the outline of the Bowen house, barely lit by the stars that peeked through the overcast sky. Somewhere in the Confederate line, its owner watched nervously to see if flames would consume his home after the Federal army departed. Short flashes of light came and went as doors opened and closed on the farmhouse. Joseph sensed that Burbridge had arrived and was holding a council of war.

"It's a new moon and cloudy," Joseph finally replied to Zachariah. "I don't expect Burbridge to come up here tonight, but they'll probably try to probe us some. They'll be comin' up that hill by daylight; you can count on it."

"You know, I could draw a bead on those lights and I might just kill me a bluecoat," Zachariah said, squinting down the barrel of his musket.

"Yeah, and the whole God damn Union Army'd open fire on us," Joseph replied. "Just keep your hands off that trigger. You'll get your chance soon enough."

In the Bowen house, now rapidly filling with smoke from his commanders' cigars, Burbridge sat down to receive reports from elements of his army.

"Jeffersonville was abandoned, sir," one of his colonels told him. "Barely a soul in the town."

"They're hoping we won't set the torch to it," he replied with a grin. "But we'll call on them after we demolish the saltworks."

"Shall I order the men to make camp, sir? The boys are pretty much give out and hungry."

"No," he replied firmly. "No fires. We have not the time and not all the men have come up yet. We'll camp when we are in striking distance of Saltville. Get them in battle line tonight and we will storm the ridge at daybreak."

He could see the disappointment and fatigue in his officers' faces, but he ignored them. "Now where is my artillery?" he demanded.

Throughout the night, Burbridge consolidated his army for the attack on Clinch Mountain. He had force-marched his men from Pikeville and pushed his troops over dangerous roads, losing horses and men to snipers and the dangerous ravines that yawned in the darkness. He did not stop to retrieve them; if they were too injured to continue, they would be only numbers added to the casualties he would report when he returned victoriously to Lexington.

A pale glow was beginning to edge above the eastern rim of the valley as the Confederates, weary from lack of sleep but energized by the surety of the coming fight, awaited their foe. Some of the men, including Zachariah, had gone out beyond the line during the night to answer the call of nature, leaving certain presents for the Union troops when they arrived. He was adjusting his suspenders as he resumed his place on the edge of the mountain road beside Joseph.

"Let's see how they like slidin' in shit when they get here," he said, as the mutter from the opposite side increased with each streak of dawn. He could hear angry men shouting orders and wagons moving on the narrow roads.

"There's a swarm of them, Joe," he said to his friend. "They're goin' to hit us hard."

"That they will, old friend," Joseph replied grimly. "That they will."

Suddenly, the remaining darkness of Thompson Valley disappeared as a thousand Federal muskets began twinkling like a riot of fireflies. For an instant, Joseph was not sure where the lights were coming from until the bullets tore into the trees above him like the winds of a giant storm, with the thunder following an instant later.

"They'll hang your young ass, yet," Elisha said to his startled son. George had just arrived at the cabin and was unsaddling his horse in the small barn, as his father materialized in the early light of dawn.

"Pappy!" George croaked, his mouth suddenly dry. "How'd you . . . "

"Fool," Elisha scowled. "We been watching you all the way. How do you think you made it here without getting' shot?"

"Pappy, I ain't goin' back this time. I'm goin' to stay up here 'til it's over."

"You're goin' to stay here, all right," Elisha said. "But as soon as that army comes back through here, you're getting' back in line in the dark the same way you got out. You just better hope no one misses you in all the ruckus."

"No, sir, I ain't . . . "

"Shut up, fool, and listen to me. If the Yankees knock down the saltworks, it will be over soon. If they don't, it could be another year. Either way, you got to go back. There's spies and scalawags all over the place. They'd sell their soul for a plug nickel and turn you in for a penny. The Union's goin' to win this, no matter what happens in Saltville, and Lord help anyone on the wrong side when it's over."

George glared at his father, but knew he could not penetrate the icy resolve in his father's eyes. Nor could he deny his father's logic, but he would not accept it. He turned to put the saddle back on his horse. There had to be somewhere he could hide.

"Leave the horse alone, George," Elisha said. "I'll send the Indians up to get you when the army comes back."

George stood motionless, afraid to defy his father and afraid not to. He had to get to Victoria somehow. He had to let her know he would not be part of the river of death that was flowing toward her father.

"Will you send word . . . ?" George began.

"Don't worry about Victoria, either," his father said, reading his mind. "Go on in the cabin. Belle left you somethin' to eat."

Elisha turned away and walked out of the tiny barn. Figures in the mist formed around him then disappeared, and George was alone again. He suddenly felt hollow and hungry, as if he had not eaten for weeks, and with slumping shoulders, he walked over to the cabin. Through the window, he could see a dim light from a single candle burning in the darkness.

He opened the door and could see food on the table and a woman standing beside the darkened hearth. At first, he thought it was his sister rushing toward him, but when he reached for her and she buried her face against his chest, he knew it was Victoria.

"Sweet Jesus, Joe," said Zachariah. "Look at those horses."

At the bottom of the hill, a white horse regiment of Union troops formed a massive line and began moving regally toward the Confederate position. Firing stopped momentarily as the entire brigade paused to look at the majestic line twisting up the hillside fields like a great white snake, coiling and straightening as it moved. Joseph had never seen anything more beautiful in his life.

As the Union column came into range, a massive fusillade burst from the tree line, tumbling a dozen blue cavalrymen from their saddles amid rearing horses whose white hair formed a chaste contrast to the sinister red flowers erupting on their bodies. Some fell with legs shot in two and struggled to right themselves amid the hail of bullets. The lucky ones fell dead immediately. Joseph cursed the Yankee soldiers for sending such horses to their doom and took aim on one that made it up on three legs, its fourth hanging by a shred of muscle. Its head flew back as the bullet found its mark and it fell back motionless. That may be the only shot I will be proud of in this God damned war, he thought.

The charge of the white horse regiment failed, and after the survivors stumbled back to the Federal line, Burbridge knew that his enemy was not afraid. He calmly ordered his foot soldiers to advance up the mountain, trading the precision of a cavalry attack for the sheer blundering weight of thousands of bodies. As he watched his men fall and tumble back down the hill, he smiled, concluding that there were not as many muskets on the other side as he had feared. His mountain howitzers belched sporadically, although his gunners had little to target. Occasionally, trees would fall, but amid the cacophony of the battle, he could not determine if any of the Rebels were crushed under them. But the action satisfied him, and as the sun arced across the valley, he calmly smoked his cigar as if watching a dance.

By late afternoon, the blue lines were making progress, although the Confederates had budged from few of their positions. Joseph's troops were calmly loading and firing as ammunition bearers ran from tree to tree, delivering bullets and cartridges. Joseph had just reloaded and was beginning to take aim when a courier ran down the line ordering the men to break off the fight and retreat.

Incredulous, Joseph turned to the young man and spat. " What? That's horseshit!" he cried. "Those bluebellies can't make it up this hill."

The courier, a young Pike County boy, flushed when Joseph exploded.

"They ain't hardly touched us." Joseph's rage was apparent. "We'll kill 'em all if they don't back off. Shit!"

But the courier had his orders and hunkered down to alert the rest of the line, receiving much the same reaction throughout his dangerous journey.

"What'd he say, Joe?" Zachariah asked as he paused to reload his weapon.

"We got to pull out," Joseph said sullenly. "Orders from the top."

"What? This is the best place we could be. It's a solid wall."

"I know that, but orders is orders. Get the boys ready to move. Son of a bitch! *Son of a bitch!*" Bullets still whizzed by them as the men gathered up their gear and waited for the signal to move.

The lovers did not answer when Dorcus knocked softly on the cabin door. Thinking they were out, she opened the door and walked in. She was bringing them more food, cornbread and buttermilk and some bacon, for she expected them to be hungry. When she opened the door, she heard George snoring peacefully and she smiled wryly as Victoria attempted to replace the apron that had fallen from her dress.

George awoke and attempted to act nonchalant, getting up to put some more wood on the fire. When the three of them sat down to eat, none of them spoke of the battle that was surely raging in Virginia, but talked only of domestic things, as if there were no other world but Greasy Creek. The geese were gone and a lot of the stock had disappeared, Dorcus told him, especially after they let them out into the woods, but at least gardens had been good this year, for which everyone was thankful.

"Aunt Haley's had another baby," Dorcus revealed. "She had a right hard time of it and she ain't doin' good . . . Daddy's worried about her, but he don't say nothin'. You know Lige." But she received only mutters in reply; George and Victoria rarely looked her way and focused their eyes on each other.

After a while, Dorcus knew it was time to leave and got up from the table. She embraced her brother and her cousin, who had always been her best friend, and started for the door. The couple protested her leaving, but only politely. It was apparent to Dorcus they had other things on their minds. Rejuvenated by the sparse meal she had provided for them, the lovers were already blushing at the thought of being alone again, and Dorcus envied them. Again, she would leave them to their own devices.

All through the night the Federals pushed them. They did not stop when they reached the line where Joseph and his boys had resisted so bravely, although Joseph could hear the cheers that went up from the Union troops when they found it abandoned.

"Let 'em have it, by God," he said to Zachariah as they rode away. "Guess we didn't want it no way."

Across Clinch Mountain was a much smaller valley with another ridge on the other side; only this time there were huge gaps in the mountain and Joseph could see the danger immediately. Laurel Gap was narrow, but it was too low to defend against the hordes of Yankee troopers he had seen coming up the Clinch. If Burbridge massed his troops against the Gap, he could easily break through the ragged band of Confederates that awaited him. If they made it, the brigade would have the river at its back and the bluecoats could cut it in two.

Even worse, Breckinridge had not yet made it to Saltville and only a few soldiers had trickled into the town. Although only a few of Trimble's men had been wounded, the loss of any soldier on this day would be keenly felt. Joseph cursed whoever made the decision to abandon Clinch Mountain. It had to come from some shitass general, he thought. Trimble would never have given up on his own.

A strange sense of dread began to churn in the pit of his stomach, but Joseph would not reveal it to Zachariah. Instead, they sat on their horses and waited for orders. Presently, Colonel Trimble rode up with another officer, followed by a group of old men and young boys from the Sixty-fourth Virginia. It was one of the last of the local regiments that had been formed and there were very few among them who had any real training in soldiering.

"Damn, is that all they got?" Zachariah whispered to his friend.

"Joseph, take these men of the Sixty-fourth and position yourself on that side of the Gap," he said, pointing to the tree-covered mountain on the left. "There are no noncoms available to lead them and I need your help here. The enemy may have crossed through on up the river and our orders are to reconnoiter."

"Yes, sir," Joseph replied immediately, although he did not look forward to leading men he did not know, especially smooth-cheeked boys and old men who used their rifles as walking sticks. Moreover, his heart fell when he realized Trimble was not going to order Zachariah to stay with him.

"The rest of you men come with me," Trimble ordered, and the riders turned to follow their commander up the valley.

"This ain't no good, Joe," Zachariah said as wheeled his horse around to face his friend. "You be God damn careful up there. You think you're goin' to get surrounded, you skedaddle."

"I'll watch my ass," Joseph replied with a grin. "Since you won't be here to watch it for me." Then he turned to his new charges. "Boys, we'll ride up that path and tie up the horses just below the point. Don't want to get any of them shot if we have to roll out of here in a hurry."

Joseph introduced himself to the squad as they began their climb and tried to learn their names. He knew he would need the information if he had to make a report after the battle. When they reached their new posts, he positioned the men as best he could and settled down to wait for the Federals to arrive. He realized he had not eaten a bite since Zachariah offered him some cheese the day before. Aside from a few gulps of water from his canteen, he had little to quell the complaints he heard from his stomach. He pulled a piece of jerky out of his pocket to chew on while he waited.

He had barely finished his meager dinner when he heard movement in the trees below him. More sounds came from beside and above him and he was shocked when a mass of bluecoats appeared. He knew he was in trouble.

Burbridge had seen the same opportunity as had Joseph; if he attacked the Gap straight on, he would face a determined enemy in a confined space and still did not know how many men awaited him. But if he took the sides of the Gap, he could fire down on the Rebels and break up their lines. Although Trimble had assigned Joseph a position that he thought would not be attacked directly, Burbridge was sending an entire regiment to take that very spot. Joseph's dozen men would face a hundred times that number.

Before he could give the order to abandon their positions, half the troops Joseph commanded left their posts at the first sound of footsteps crackling in the bushes and the remainder fired their rounds into the dense forest and ran. Only the boy to his right stayed with Joseph, as much afraid of the revolver Joseph had drawn as the Yankees that were rapidly surrounding them.

"Get back to the horses," he ordered and the boy dropped his musket and ran. Joseph emptied the chambers of his weapon to cover him and then turned to follow the petrified youth. He stopped in his tracks and froze, as if he had just stumbled onto a pit of vipers. In front of him were three Federal troopers with bayonets extended and hammers cocked. Beside them, the frightened young man was ghastly pale and shook in his fear as a Union bayonet pointed at his throat. One of the men spoke:

"Hold on there, Secesh," he said. "You ain't goin' nowhere. Gimme that hogleg before I blow your damn head off."

Joseph dropped his revolver and raised his arms. The woods came alive with soldiers, it seemed, and all of them head their muskets pointed directly at him. There was no place to run; he was now a prisoner.

That evening, he sat leaning back against a wagon wheel with his hands bound behind him, along with a half-dozen other boys who had been captured before the Federals went into camp. Although the Union force had mostly Kentuckians in its ranks, the general had expressly ordered the prisoners to be held by the Michigan boys, who he thought would be less likely to allow the Confederate Kentucky boys to slip away. The Thirty-ninth, in fact, had been strictly forbidden to speak to them. The Yankees were cooking their evening meals and Joseph was famished, but neither he nor any of the prisoners had been offered anything to eat or drink. Neither had they been given a chance to relieve themselves, and some of them had wet their own pants, the result less of bladder pressure than of fear, especially by the young boys who had just lived through their first battle.

Joseph saw the Union commander, illuminated by the campfires, ride up to the small prison camp and speak to the guards. He strained to listen, but could not hear what was said amid the clatter of five thousand men preparing and eating their suppers and belching and farting and snoring as they began to fall asleep. After Burbridge left, one of the guards walked over to him and spoke: "You got it made, Reb. The general says he wants to take you boys back to Lexington with him." Somehow that gave him no comfort, but exhaustion overtook him and he eventually fell asleep. It seemed he had slept for only a few minutes before the drums awakened him.

Below the Union camp, at the barricades in front of Saltville, Zachariah could hear them resounding off the canyon walls long before the first troops came into view. He could even hear the playing of a fife. He grudgingly admired the precise cadence the Federal army was providing its men. We're lucky to have a God damn bugle, he thought bitterly. Hope Joe's enjoying the music out there.

"Listen to that shit," he remarked to the soldier beside him, another Pike County boy. "They're tryin' to scare us off this hill." The other soldier merely winced.

"If they make that much racket now, it's goin' to be a pretty loud show today," Zachariah said, attempting to put up a brave front for the young man nervously crouched beside him. "If I go deaf and can't hear mess call, you let me know."

As the brigade waited for the fight to begin, all the men made such small talk, brave talk, or sometimes just silly talk in their quiet terror. But for the most part, the troops were ready for the fight, especially the Tenth. It had seen the first of the fighting and had been on the front line steadily as the battle unfolded. It had lost very few men: no one killed, a few wounded and even fewer captured. But among them was Joseph Hopkins. Just the best man in this whole God damned army, Zachariah thought.

But while the brigade and the new troops knew this was a desperate fight, the Tenth itself was even more motivated. It had been placed at the center of the action because it asked for it. They were not fighting for the saltworks or Jeff Davis or the South or even for Virginia. They were fighting to get back their prisoners, to get Joe back. Their horses were tied up just behind the hill they were defending so they could reach them easily when the blue lines broke. They had a score to settle and they were all grimly determined to settle it. The men did not plan to remain in defensive positions for long. Colonel Trimble was still mounted, however, and splashed through the placid stream in front of his men, shouting encouragement and vengeance. The battle was ready to begin.

"Here they come," someone shouted as the first of the Federal columns marched onto the field. With bayonets glistening, regiment after regiment filed onto the field across the stream opposite the Tenth's position. Until now, the Confederates had not seen how large the Federal army really was. Even at the Bowen Farm, which sat on top of one of the gentle hills of Thompson Valley, much of the army was in reserve and did not take part in the attack on Clinch Mountain. Now the sinister thing drew up in from of them like a nightmarish snake preparing to strike. "Shit," Zachariah said to his comrade. "This may not be so easy after all."

"You reckon we could live here?" Victoria asked him. "After it's all over?"

She did not say "war" to George, whose Federal uniform hung on a wooden peg on the wall of the cabin.

"I don't see why not," he replied. "Pap'd let us have it, and he and Uncle Joe built it when they was boys. I remember him sayin' that they had to build a cabin to keep the land, and Granpap said they couldn't do it. It 'bout killed both of 'em, but they did it all themselves. Pap lived here first with Mam, but it got a little crowded when we came along."

"Not to mention Aunt Sally," she laughed. "Or Aunt Haley."

It's good to hear her laugh, George thought, there's been so little to laugh over all these years. He pressed his lips to her hands, now roughened by too much hard work, work that men used to do before the War came and took them all away, but George thought that he had never felt anything so soft in his life. He looked into her eyes and silently swore he would never go away again. He could not swear to her out loud, not yet. He had to find a way to tell his father that nothing on earth would make him leave this hilltop.

The first explosions from the Confederate guns took a heavy toll on the massed troops who began their steady walk across the field. Huge holes appeared in the closely packed lines as arms and legs rained down on the troops still advancing. Smoke rapidly covered the field, but Zachariah could still see what the Confederate guns and muskets were doing to the Union line. At nearly point-blank range, it was a turkey shoot. The first advance fell apart and the Federals began to back away.

"Watch 'em run! Watch 'em run!" Giddy shouts went up across the Confederate line as Zachariah calmly reloaded and waited for the next wave. He felt sweat running down the side of his face and he lifted his hand to his brow. Am I just hot or scared shitless, he wondered? But when he looked at his hand he saw it was not sweat he was wiping away; it was blood. He felt for his cap, which was still on his head, and breathed hard to see if he could feel a wound in his chest or stomach, but felt nothing.

"Hey Bub, are you...?" He started to question the young man beside him, but did not finish the sentence. His comrade was sitting against a sapling with his rifle partially across his lap, his right hand still on the ramming rod, the reloading stopped in mid-motion. There was a simple look of surprise on his face, which was tilted slightly, with gravity pushing down the soldier's head to fill the gap where the right side of his neck had been. He was covered in scarlet from his blouse to his crotch.

"Bless your heart, little brother," Zachariah said as he closed his friend's eyes with his sooty hands and turned back to the battle.

"Here they come again!" someone said and once more the thunder rolled.

"Hey Zach, can you see anything?" one of the men asked him. "I can't see for shit."

"Just keep shootin'," Zachariah yelled back. "You'll by God hit somethin'."

Again and again, the blue line surged forward and fell back. They had almost made it to the top of one of the hills to the right of the Tenth, but the intensity of the fire drove them back. Men fell on both sides with eyes blown out, arms shot in two, and legs buckled after balls smashed into bones and joints, but the Confederates were still giving more than they got. From a high point on the ridge facing the

Confederate line, Burbridge was furious. His fine troops could not move the ruffians in front of him and, even worse, he could hear their taunts. "Come and get you some salt, you shit-eaters," they yelled. "Makes a right tasty turd."

The fighting was so close that some of the Rebels were throwing rocks at their opponents and each wave Burbridge sent forward was repulsed.

"Send in the coloreds and the Thirty-ninth," he ordered. "Let's see what those savages do about that."

In lockstep with the Fifth United States Colored Troops, the Thirty-ninth Kentucky Mounted Infantry raised their muskets and marched into the blue fog encompassing the valley. As they emerged on the riverbank, directly in front of the Tenth, their opponents were mercifully unable to recognize friends or family in the blue line in front of them. Their eyes were all drawn to the black soldiers that suddenly appeared as if they were the legions of hell. Colonel Trimble may have recognized someone he knew in the blue ranks, for he had the sharp eye of a true military leader, but he told no one. He never had the chance.

As a black soldier raised his weapon and fired, the back of Trimble's head erupted in a fountain of gore and he fell dead into the stream as his horse bolted and ran away. For the briefest of moments, the entire Confederate line stopped firing and then with angry shouts that could be heard above the indescribable roar and reverberation of cannon and musket fire off the valley walls, the enraged gray line of the Tenth Kentucky surged out of its positions to take the battle to the enemy. Officers ordered their men back at gunpoint, only because they had been given orders not to attack under any circumstances. One word from their commanders and they would have launched themselves into the middle of the Federal ranks and taken an even more dreadful toll.

But their defense was enough, and after the final Union charge failed, the line moved back to safety. In the short fall day, darkness was beginning to cover the valley and only sporadic firing could be heard as both sides husbanded their ammunition. Soon only the moaning of the wounded could be heard as the battlefield writhed like rats under a carpet. Neither side came out to collect its wounded, although the lifeless body of Colonel Trimble was reverently carried out of the stream before the final charge was made. Those who remembered that night would not speak of the blasphemies they heard from the dying, but they would remember one cry heard over and over; one word, little more than a question, that came from blue and gray alike: "Mama?"

By daybreak there were no more sounds from the battlefield and no more Union soldiers behind it. Burbridge had ordered large bonfires to be built, to trick the Confederates into believing there would be another fight in the morning, but slipped away during the night.

He took his prisoners with him.

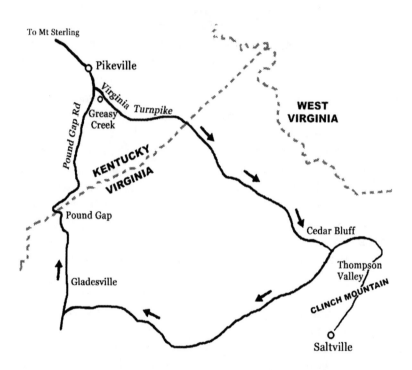

Route of Burbridge's Attack and Retreat

Like Breckinridge three years before, Burbridge detoured up the Virginia Turnpike instead of advancing along the better Mt. Sterling-Pound Gap road. However, after his defeat, he returned to Kentucky by the more expedient route through Pound Gap.

"Army's comin' back, son," Elisha said. "You got to get goin'."

"Paw, I ain't goin' . . ." George began to reply, but his father cut him off.

"Shut up and listen to me. They caught Joe; he's a prisoner."

George felt as if his father had hit him square in the heart with a maul. He knew prisoner exchanges had been suspended and Joseph would rot in a northern prison until the War ended.

"You got to watch out for him as long as you can," Elisha continued. "You make sure he's got a blanket so he won't freeze to death in one of those northern hellholes."

"Yes, sir," George said meekly, with all his plans for resistance now evaporated.

The Indian boy walked up to the cabin with George's horse already saddled. Dorcus came out of the cabin and embraced her brother; he could hear Victoria crying softly inside.

"Go tell her goodbye, brother," she said. "She knows."

I'll do what Pappy told me to do, George thought, but as soon as they send Uncle Joe up north, I'll quit this God damn war forever, and I'll die before I let anything else hurt her.

Little over a month had passed since Joseph was captured and the day had finally come for the last of the battle's casualties to be recorded; he would be the last one to fall. It was cold on this November 7, and the water seeped through his rotted shoes as he stepped down from the wagon with the other two men. They had not been at Saltville, but they listened as Joseph told them of the Yankees' inglorious defeat.

He could see children in the crowd that had been assembled on orders from General Burbridge. Their frightened faces reminded him of his own children. The last time he had seen them was when they had desperately broken through the Yankee column to try to touch their father as he stumbled, bound at the wrist, across his own farm with the other men who had been captured. He remembered troopers shooting into the ground in front of his family, to make them go back. He remembered his wife sinking to her knees in the cold remains of the cotton field and the children flocking to her.

Why did they make these children come out here, he wondered? Children shouldn't have to see something like this. It ain't right.

"LEFT FACE!" the Union sergeant bellowed as the soldiers assembled in front of him. "FRONT RANK KNEEL."

Joseph scanned the crowd one last time and was pleased that the townspeople of Bloomfield were shouting encouragement, in spite of threats leveled against them by the soldiers. He had never been to their fair village before, and he regretted he would not have the opportunity to thank them for their kindness today. Apparently, today's event was not something new to these folks. Almost all the women were sobbing and the men all had clenched fists, which they often raised in rage at the soldiers who had been herding the prisoners like cattle.

"Blackguards!" they yelled. "It's you that should be shot."

Joseph and the two men beside him declined blindfolds; they wanted to look into the eyes of the men facing them. They did not listen to the Federal sergeant stumble over the orders he was reading; instead they stood erect and waited for what was to come. The crowd was moaning now in protest. A Union lieutenant rode up to them and ordered quiet, but they ignored him.

"PREPARE TO FIRE!"

Joseph began to whisper the names of his wife and children: Lucinda, my bride, he said. Take care of them. Victoria; Polly; Elizabeth; Louisa; John Miles, my fine boy; Aura Lee; America; Angeline. Lucinda, Victoria, Polly, Elizabeth, Louisa, John Miles, Aura Lee, America, Angeline. Lucinda, Victoria, Polly, Elizabeth, Louisa, John Miles, Aura Lee, America, Angeline . . .

"TAKE YOUR AIM!"

He had almost enough time to speak their names a fourth time, and had gotten almost to the end of his list when he could sense his comrades looking at him quizzically when he said "America."

"Wha . . . ?" one of the men started to ask.

"FIRE!"

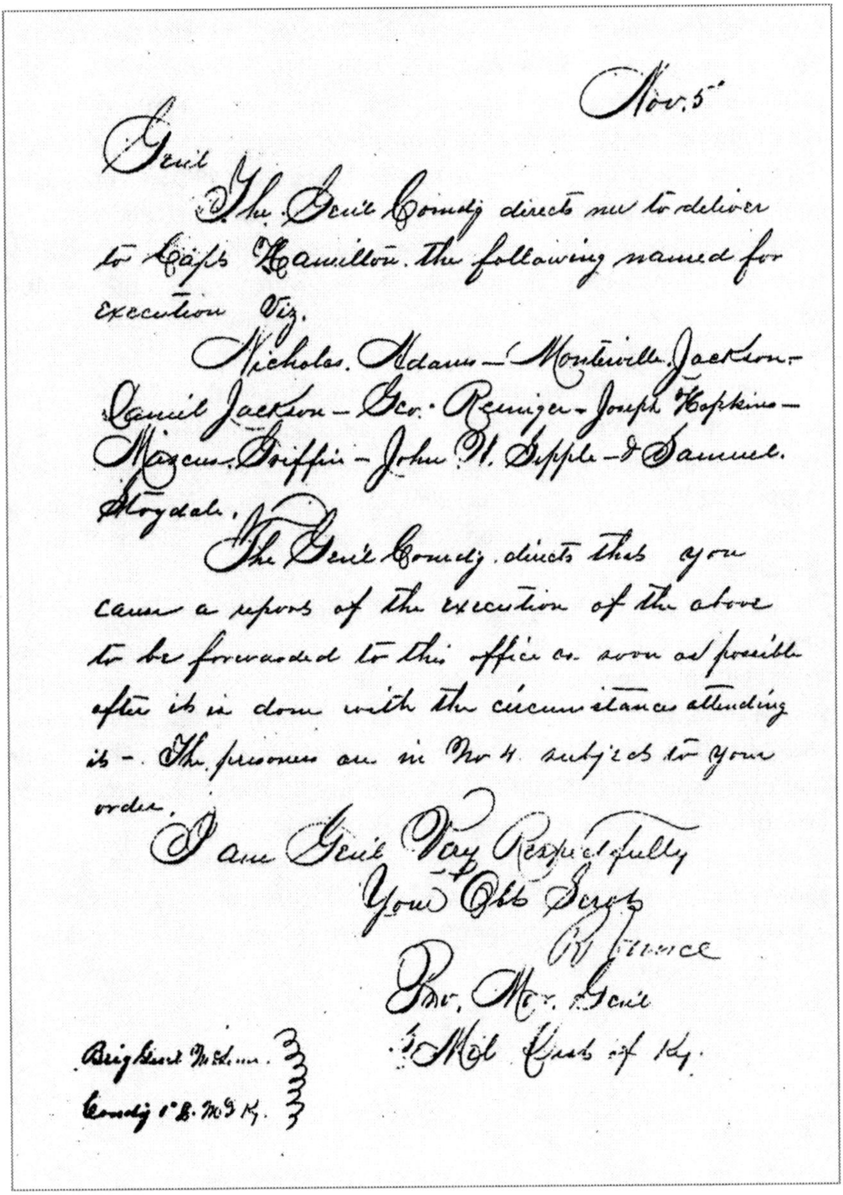

Nov. 5

Gen'l

The Gen'l Comdg directs me to deliver to Capt Hamilton the following named for execution Viz.

Nicholas Adams — Monteville Jackson — Daniel Jackson — Geo. Reninger — Joseph Hopkins — Marcus Griffin — John H. Sipple — & Samuel Stoydale.

The Gen'l Comdg directs that you cause a report of the execution of the above to be forwarded to this office as soon as possible after it is done with the circumstances attending it — The prisoners are in No 4 subject to your order.

I am Gen'l Very Respectfully
Your Obt Servt
[illegible]
Pro. Mar. Genl
Mil Dist of Ky.

Brig Genl McLean
Comdg 1st D. M D Ky.

Joseph Hopkins' Execution Order

Word had already come to the farms on Greasy Creek and Shelby Creek by December, when George deserted for the last time as the Federal troops again advanced on Saltville. His father met him at the cabin on Ripley Knob and brought him some civilian clothes to wear. He would not require George to return to the army this time, although George returned on his own a month later, after he determined he could not face Victoria in his shame. He was court-martialed when he returned and sent to the stockade for a month, only to catch dysentery from the other men in the stockade. He was transferred to the hospital where he served his time and was sent back to his unit just as word came of Appomattox.

The Thirty-ninth Kentucky did not muster out then, but was kept on duty until September, chasing renegades and bandits who were still loose in the mountains. George contracted measles in August while camping in Pike County and was sent home to recover. He did not make it back to the regiment before orders came for the Thirty-ninth to disband.

Elisha knew of Joseph's death long before the family heard the news, however. Dorcus said that the day Joseph died the whippoorwills launched into song and continued throughout the evening and night. Before dark, the Indian boy came to Elisha's farm to tell him to come with him, that the elders wanted to speak to him, and Elisha left. Later that night, she saw the light from a great fire on Ripley Knob and could hear her father's voice chanting with the Indians.

Just after daylight the next morning, she saw him return, slump-shouldered and drawn. She saw him walk directly to Haley's cabin, where she had been waiting for him. He went inside and shut the door.

Chapter Six

Darkness

The first of them came home after Appomattox; they were the Pike County boys who would not wait for Kentucky to join the rest of the South, the boys who had gone east in their restlessness and impatience, and joined regiments that began forming when word came of Fort Sumter. When they returned, they were not the fresh-faced plowboys who had departed in the sure and certain knowledge that they would return as heroes, who had left their mountain homes with laughter and bravado. They had gone to the east and to the west as mere boys and returned as old men, sick and heartsick, weighed down with memories of too many nights on cold ground, too many burials on hot summer days, and too many friends who would never ride with them again. Some of the boys who went west now came from the east, lost from their dying army in Tennessee, and pushed out of Georgia, until its final death in the foothills of North Carolina.

The Union boys were coming home too, but their receptions were no more celebratory than those of the defeated Confederates. They were better clothed and had been better fed and even had their mustering-out pay in real money lining their pockets, but their homecomings were like all mountain homecomings: fearful and anguished, and they were no better prepared than their Confederate brethren for what awaited them.

Dorcus saw practically all the Greasy Creek boys who came back; at least those who could or would. She saw them walk by Elisha's farm, hollow-eyed, to the families they left behind, some who would welcome them back and some who would not. Some of them left again, in tears or in rage, and she would add them to the roster of the dead; additional casualties of the War that never seemed to end. Some of the boys, in faded blue shirts or tattered butternut, would make their way to Elisha to seek his help in dispelling their nightmares and exorcising their demons, as they reckoned his whiskey to be the only thing that could provide relief. Eventually only Zachariah remained unaccounted for.

From her window, she could see Clarinda's cabin, now quiet again, except for the sounds of the children, whose voices had been supplanted too long by the drunken laughter of strangers. Every day she could see Clarinda pause from her labor as another walking scarecrow stumbled up the road by her farm, and every night she could see Clarinda stand in her doorway, silhouetted by candlelight, and wait for her husband to return. And late into the night, she could see Clarinda reluctantly close the door after another hellish day of waiting for her man. Dorcus wondered what she would say, what she could say, to Zachariah when he came home, if he ever did.

Clarinda was not the only woman to have done whatever was necessary to save her children and Zack would not be the only man to return to a family he no longer knew, for no one was the same now. Only in the most private conversations would anyone speak of the War, like it was an ugly dream, too vile and shameful to reveal, but neither could they speak of the years before it began. It was as if a dark veil had fallen over Greasy Creek that summer, an opaque screen that obscured the past, if not hiding it altogether, a barrier erected by the people themselves to keep them from remembering, because all they had was an uncertain future and a present that was cloudy and dark, like the cold days of winter, but not nearly so forgiving.

"He'll be back soon," Clarinda would tell Dorcus. "My man will come home and we'll start all over again." Dorcus hoped it would be true.

"By God," Zachariah whispered reverently to his comrades. "That's Jeff Davis himself."

The president of the Confederate States of America nodded regally as he rode by on his great black mare, accompanied by grim-faced Confederate officers. After all these years, Zachariah could see the very symbol of what he had given so much for, and he was full of pride. He had expected Davis to be as ragged as the tiny army that protected him, but the president sat firm in his saddle and the sheer dignity of the man flowed along with him like the wind.

What remained of the Tenth Kentucky and other remnants of the Southwest Virginia Brigade were lined up on their horses, in something approximating military order, after the word had passed that a "high-ranking" official would be joining the wagon train. For several days, the boys of the Tenth had guarded the last vestiges of the Confederate government as it made its way from Danville, Virginia into North Carolina in what everyone seemed to know would be a futile attempt to escape the hordes of blue-coated soldiers that were approaching from the North and the South.

These were the last days, Zachariah knew, but he was here. Joseph was gone, Trimble was gone, Morgan had been shot in the back in Tennessee even before then, and now the great Army of Northern Virginia had passed into history. The Southwest Virginia Brigade had answered the call from Lee barely a month before: his lines were overextended and he would be abandoning Petersburg and Richmond to move what was left of his army to ground of his choosing to fight Grant. General Basil Duke, Morgan's brother-in-law, had taken command of the Southwest Virginia District after Breckinridge was called to Richmond to become the last Secretary of War for the Confederacy. Duke gave orders for the brigade to pack up and move; any supplies not transportable were to be hidden or burned, and any families accompanying their husbands in camp were to be sent home. The brigade would never return to Saltville, and Home Guards would assume the responsibility of protecting the saltworks and lead mines and even the headquarters at Abingdon.

Duke led his men to the east, out of the hills, and there was a swagger to the troops as they rode, like in the old days when the regiments were strong, and they could almost feel the ghosts of their comrades, riding spectral horses beside them. They were mountain men, tough and resilient, used to hard times, but it was not just for Lee they marched; it was a final vindication of all their sacrifice, a final chance at a great battle where they would be noted and remembered, the last shot they would ever have at redemption and glory.

But it was not to be.

By the time the 650-odd men of the Southwest Virginia Brigade arrived in Christiansburg, they met Lee's soldiers going home.

The same thoughts jumped electrically through the riders as they rushed toward each other with the news: Lee's surrendered! The War is over! We're going home! Through tear-filled eyes they made the argument to each other: if Lee had surrendered, there was no reason to fight any longer. Without Lee, there was no Army and there was no Confederacy.

But the War was not over.

There was still a fight coming between Union General William T. Sherman and Confederate General Joseph E. Johnston somewhere in North Carolina, and there was still an intact Confederate army in Texas. Duke saw the sudden restlessness of the men and attempted to rally them to turn south for the coming fight between Sherman and Johnston, but few joined him. The commanders of the skeletal regiments that remained would not send their men into another battle; in spite of Duke's entreaties they started back to the mountains, to find what was left of their farms and families, to try to rebuild their lives.

Major George Diamond, who had taken over command of the Tenth Kentucky after Trimble's death, wanted to go with Duke, but Giltner, his commander, ordered the entire command to start home. However, at the first encampment, Diamond approached Giltner with a request for permission to leave the command and follow Duke. Reluctantly, Giltner gave his assent, and Diamond, along with about ninety men, rode out of the sullen camp. Zachariah was among them. In his mind, he had no home to return to.

After rejoining Duke, the ragtag Kentuckians intercepted the Confederate government wagon train just across the Virginia border in North Carolina and immediately became its guard. Not long afterward, word came that Johnston had surrendered as well, but the boys stayed on as the wagon train pushed on through the mountains, even after they received their pay. It was the first payroll in months and the last they would receive as Confederate soldiers, and it was in gold.

A few days later, the family of Jefferson Davis joined the procession, and now the president was here, Jeff Davis himself, under their protection. Zachariah jangled the Mexican coins in his pocket and pulled them out to look more closely at them.

After all we done, this is what we have to show for it, he thought. Money from another country. It ain't enough. There ain't enough to pay for what we went through.

Yet he was still there, ready to fight to the death. He wondered if anybody would take Mexican gold if he tried to buy anything. He wondered if he would live to spend it.

"They say John Cabell is out there somewhere," one of the men whispered to Zachariah. "They say he's the only one left that has any sense in this shitass war. Just where in hell are we goin', Zack?"

Zachariah started to answer, but was interrupted before he uttered a word. The same officers who had accompanied Davis, including Major Diamond, rode up to face the company.

No, God damn it, Zachariah thought. They're going to quit. I know that look. It's finished and they're sending us home.

"Gentlemen," one of the officers began. He was almost shouting so that all the men could hear him. "As you know, General Johnston has been forced to capitulate and the entire Federal army has been loosed upon us. Our numbers are not sufficient to withstand the attacks that will surely come."

No, no, no. It can't be over.

"Our responsibility now, "the officer continued, "is to ensure the safety of President Davis as he makes his way to join General Smith in Texas. Consequently, we will disband this organization here."

Zachariah's pounding heart fell as he heard the words and a universal groan went through the ranks.

"However," the officer went on. "We have obtained a plan to throw the enemy off the president's trail. We will disperse in haste in various directions, as if we are guarding someone and, with the help of Providence, lure them away from the president and his family."

But if everybody skedaddles, who's going to protect the president?

Then the officer spoke again: "I have been asked to select ten worthy men to guard the president in his journey. This will be a hazardous mission, as you well know, and I will select only volunteers. Should any of you wish this assignment, please come . . ."

Before the officer could finish his sentence, the entire company spurred their horses to cover the short distance between them, and in the midst of the confusion, Zachariah vowed that if he were not selected, he would follow anyway. He would follow Jefferson Davis to hell itself, which in his estimation would be only slightly worse that what he had left behind or what awaited him in Kentucky.

For the first time in her life, Dorcus was truly exhausted. It wasn't the work; she had always worked, had always done both men's and women's jobs, even more so after the men went away. She could plow the fields or raise a hog for scraping as easily as any man, but she was tired, bone-tired all the time. With all her other duties, it fell to her to assume even more. She had to take care of Grandpap and Mam, who were old and feeble now, and worse since Joseph died.

Her Aunt Haley had never fully recovered her health after the birth of her last child, although it was not the birth that had sickened her. Something else was ravaging her body and she could feel part of her dying every day.

"You take my babies and raise them when I go," she told Dorcus. "You got to do that for me, Belle."

"Hush, woman, you're goin' to get better," Dorcus tried to reassure her.

"No, I'm not, and it'll be hard on your daddy. You make sure he eats."

"That's fool talk, Haley." Dorcus had long dropped the appellation of 'Aunt,' and in many ways Mahala had become a sister to her or even a daughter.

"I got to go home, Belle. I got to make peace with my family. They hate me and I can't die like that."

"You ain't goin' to die, I tell you."

"Belle, I love you like a sister, but you can't lie worth a damn. Just take care of my babes and tell them their mother is an angel when they ask you." She paused and caught her breath. "But I 'spect I'll have to settle for second-hand wings."

Her father was worried. Elisha himself was worn out; staying up at night guarding the little stock they still had from people he would have once happily given a lamb or a brace of chickens. But it was not just the thievery and privation that enervated him; it was the losses to his family they had already suffered and the losses they would yet endure. Elisha was not accustomed to helplessness.

There was Clarinda, raising a child who was not Zachariah's and praying for the day he would come home so that she could make it up to him. Not a day passed that she would not send for Dorcus, to ask for help with a sick child or to help manage the remnants of Zachariah's farm.

Lucinda sent for her for the same reasons, and Dorcus made regular trips across the mountain to check on the now fatherless family and the daughter whose belly was now swelling with George's child. She was the surrogate father and mother for both families, and she had never known the embrace of a man.

Oftentimes, she would go out into the woods alone, and hide behind the great trees to sit and weep, to cast off the fiends that haunted her, so that she could go back to her labors. I'm doing all this, she would think, and I am growing old before my time. When will I have a chance at marriage and a family? Will I have a chance? Will there be any man left for me? Will I grow old with no one to take care of me as I have taken care of others? But she would finish crying and wipe her eyes and go back to work.

It was all she could do.

Somehow Zachariah persuaded the captain to let him go along with the president as a scout. He would not be part of the regular party, but would ride far ahead of the wagon train to look for danger and follow behind to throw off any pursuers with false information. One of the scribes had forged him an officer's parole from Johnston's army, so he could keep his sidearm and horse, although he fully expected both would be taken from him eventually.

But not without a fight, Zachariah thought grimly, and if it comes to that, here's as good a place to die as anywhere.

He could even be shot as a spy if his papers were proven false. But if he were not challenged, he would be able to move swiftly, alone through the hills, to reconnoiter for the president. To the people he met, he would just be another soldier going home and all eyes would turn away for fear that he might ask them for food for his journey or a place to sleep out of the wind and rain.

He had last seen the president when he reported the night before. He had heard the sounds of a skirmish and had ridden to investigate, finding two Union regiments shooting at each other in the darkness. Both sides of the fight had expected a large force surrounding the fleeing Jefferson Davis and had opened fire almost indiscriminately.

That's a good sign, he thought. They won't be looking for a little bitty outfit like us. Ol' Jeff might have a chance after all.

The captain seemed pleased with the news and walked over to the president's wagon, where he was seated with his family around a campfire. Zachariah could see him raise himself sartorially when the captain approached and listen attentively to the report. The president nodded occasionally as he listened and then turned to Zachariah with a slight bow in salutation. The evening was wet and cold, but Zachariah felt his chest swell as if he were receiving a salute on a summer parade field, and he turned his horse to strike out in the darkness. Somewhere up ahead, he would find a place to hide in the bushes and take off his horse's saddle to rest him until dawn. Then he would saddle up and ride ahead again.

He had ridden for almost an hour when he found a cow pen where his horse could graze on the spring grass as he surveyed the surrounding woods for a hiding place. He removed the bridle so the horse could eat and walked through the tree line. After he found a small cliff behind a copse of trees, he waited for his horse to finish and replaced the bridle. It obeyed reluctantly, but followed Zachariah into the woods. He tied it to a sapling and took off the saddle to use as a pillow. He wondered if Breckinridge still had the one Dorcus gave him as he drifted into sleep.

He dreamed of Texas and Greasy Creek removed to Texas and a still pure Clarinda on a Texas farm when he awakened to hoofbeats early the next morning. He could hear many soldiers and even though dawn was just beginning to streak across the sky, he knew they were headed toward the camp. He hurriedly saddled his horse and rode through the woods and fields, paralleling the road, until he neared the camp. He tied his horse to a limb and approached on foot. When he broke through the bushes, the field in front of him was awash in bluecoats racing toward the spot where he had left the president the night before. They had to be upon him, but strangely, there was no gunfire.

Zachariah spent the better part of the morning watching from concealment, and by noon he could see wagons in a column. Federal soldiers surrounded it, and Federal soldiers were driving the teams. Soon the prisoners came into view, but he could not see the president among them. His mind churned. Had he escaped? Is he lost in the woods? Could I find him? For a moment, Zachariah had visions of carrying Jefferson Davis all the way to Texas on his horse. They would make a dash for the Mississippi, find a way to get across and the president would be safe. But he was a soldier, and he could see from the way the soldiers were guarding the wagon train that they were positioned to repel attacks. They were not looking for Jefferson Davis, he realized; they had him.

It was over. It was truly over, he realized, and he crumpled in exhaustion, as if he had been carrying a bale of cotton alone, all by himself, and now it had fallen off.

He assessed his situation. He was free. He had papers; he had a horse; he even had money. He could go on to Texas if he wanted. He could go to New Orleans and blend into the crowd. Joe and Lige had been there once and they told him about it. He could find a place somewhere he could be taken in and he could live his life again without ever having to think about anything. He was free. Throughout the day he waited, his mind swirling with the choices he could make.

The patrols continued until dark and Zachariah did not move until he felt it was safe. He found his horse and began riding, again beside the road and through the brush. He found another pasture and again let his horse graze for a short time and then secured another spot where he could sleep. From here on he would ride only at night, as long as there was a moon to guide him. He had made his decision. He was heading home.

There was no other place he could go.

"You can't see him," Dorcus said to Victoria. "He's sick and you ain't goin' to go up there and get sick yourself. You just had a child, girl. You ain't well yet."

Dorcus would not let Victoria climb the mountain to Ripley Knob, where George had gone when the regiment sent him home. And for the first time, he came home legally; if he did not survive, and many did not, his death would be less paperwork for his sergeant.

"He's got measles," Dorcus continued.

"But I got to see him, Belle," Victoria protested. "He's got to know that Mam said we could marry. He's got papers. They can't report him now."

"Not yet, lady," said Dorcus. "You can see him as soon as he's better. But you ain't goin' up there till then. I can't believe you walked all the way over here with this child in your arms." Dorcus looked at the infant peacefully gurgling on the bed. "You got to save your strength for this young'un. You don't need to be wastin' away climbin' up and down these hills."

"I just wanted to see him. I want him to see Rebecca."

"He'll see her soon enough, but not until he's well." Dorcus was adamant; Victoria knew that she could not convince her otherwise.

"Then can I stay with you?" Victoria asked. "Until I can see him?"

"Just for tonight," she replied. "Tomorrow you got to go back to Shelby Creek. I'll take you myself. You ain't goin' to see that boy till he's well."

Later that night Dorcus put Victoria and the baby in her bed and slipped in behind her cousin and best friend. She put her arm around her, just like they did when they were children, when they would laugh and giggle until Phoebe shushed them, when they had dreams and hopes and had their entire lives ahead of them. Just as sleep had overtaken, Dorcus awoke with a start, realizing she was slipping into a dream. But then she remembered the dream and closed her eyes to entice it to return, pretending she had not given it up.

Not one goose, he thought. Not one goose at any farm he passed and but a precious few starving dogs to protect the cabins. Fields gone to weeds; fences broke down; folks won't come out to speak. Sweet Jesus, he asked himself, what happened here? He had seen it everywhere from Georgia to Tennessee and all through the Virginia hills to home; in so many fields the only thing new were the graves, from which nothing would ever spring again.

As a soldier, he had learned to look for good ground, places where he could fight using the land as an advantage, hillocks where redoubts could be formed, escape routes hidden in the valleys, rivers, and streams, or thick stands of trees to slow the enemy. Now he found himself looking for good ground for corn or potatoes or beans, or a spot for peas where the sun would strike in the morning and the shade come over when the day got hot. He had made himself think about farming again every day of his journey, even though it knew it would be too late to plant when he got home. By the time he got to Virginia, he had no horse anyway. It had been taken from him in Georgia, along with his pistol, by the Union troops who searched him, everywhere but his rotted boots. He limited his protest to just enough to be believed, but not enough to be thrown into the stockade, and they laughingly sent him on his way with Mexican gold under his feet.

It was dark when he arrived at Pound Gap, and he sat down on a rock to look out at Pike County. He could have been home by daylight, but he spent the night there, outside the broken-down huts that remained from the time it was fortified, when it was a crossing point between two countries, one of which no longer existed. He went inside the ramshackle structures, but there was that smell again, and it drove him away. It was not just the smell of tobacco smoke and shit and sweat, which was still there long after the men had gone home; it was a different but familiar smell. He recognized it from the battlefield, whether the corpses were fresh or not, and it remained in the air even after the dead had been committed to the ground.

He woke up as dawn was breaking, and started down Pine Mountain. By the time he got to Joseph's farm, it was noon and he stopped to look at the destruction that had been wrought upon the place. The barns had collapsed and a few chickens pecked around the yard. A weathered cow protested her hunger inside a muddy lot. No one could be seen outside the house. He could have passed by and walked on to Greasy Creek, but he wanted to see the family. At first, no one answered when he knocked, but he knew someone was inside. He had heard their voices as he walked unchallenged by goose or dog through the yard.

"Lucy," he said through the bolted door. "It's Zack." The door swung open suddenly, as if Lucy and the children expected their father to be with him, and he could see the utter despondency in their faces when they saw he was not. They had never given up hope that he would return, even though Elisha had already gone to Bloomfield to bring his body home, only to return with the news that he had found his grave, but could not distinguish it from two others, those who fell with Joseph on that awful day. But Zachariah was their father's best friend, and although his arrival reopened wounds that had never healed, could never heal, they took him in and fed him and were surprised when he asked to spend the night in what remained of the barn.

"Don't send nobody over to Clary," he begged, and they honored his request.

In the morning, he gave them half what he had in his boots and walked up Little Creek and across the old buffalo trail to the top of the hill. When he arrived at the summit, he looked down on Greasy Creek where he could see his children and his wife in the garden. He had to hold himself back to keep from running into their arms.

Dorcus was leaving her grandparents' cabin when she felt the silence. She had gone to her grandparents' cabin earlier with their breakfast, and stayed with them to make sure the old man was fed, since the elder Dorcus's hands were only a little less trembling than his. But when she came outside, she no longer heard the voices of Clarinda's children and walked over to the point to investigate. Something had stopped their chatter and she was concerned. She could see them standing motionless, as if they had all come upon a rattlesnake at the same time, but they were not backing away and their faces were turned to the old mountain road. In the distance, she could see a figure walking, a gaunt scarecrow with its hat down over its face, but she knew who it was. Her heart began to pound.

She watched the figure approach the farm. She watched the children, the boys and the girls, as they sifted through their memories, trying to recollect the image of their father, and not really believing that it was he. She watched Clarinda stumble through the corn and run toward the gate where she waited, not knowing if he would even stop. But he walked into the farm and Dorcus saw the children gather around him as Clarinda crumpled to the ground at his knees. In a moment he fell to his own knees and the children swarmed protectively around their father. For the rest of her life, Dorcus could remember that scene, remember the tears of the family, and remember the silence their welcoming shrieks had broken.

144

It was October when George and Victoria got their marriage license, and Dorcus went with them, hovering around them protectively as they walked proudly through the streets of Pikeville. They would have married long ago if George had not been a deserter with the possibility of being reported by the scalawags who hung around the courthouse in Pikeville. Many a boy had fallen prey to those Judases and had been taken away in chains. Now, with all the regiments mustered out, there was no one for them to report to, no way to make a dollar from the misfortunes of others, even though they were still there. They would always be there, Dorcus knew, lurking in the shadows, attempting to curry favor with the makeshift county government by spying on their neighbors and bearing false witness when paid to do so.

You report my brother now, you sons-of-bitches, Dorcus thought. Ain't nobody goin' to pay you anymore, are they? Nobody gives a damn about deserters now, and you sorry turds never put on a uniform, never fought for any side. Damn you all to hell.

She recognized more than a few of Elisha's customers among the surly group.

By the time they got back to Greasy Creek, Victoria's face was flushed, but she beamed at the prize she showed her family. The next day she and George would be married, at her Uncle Lum's house, and she and George would start their lives together without hiding from anyone. This was her day, she told Dorcus, she and George had waited long enough to marry and nothing would stop them now.

Dorcus at first resisted having the wedding at Columbus's, but he had pleaded with her to allow it. He wanted to do right by his brother's family, he said, and he would pay for the feast, for real flour and sugar for the pies and cakes, for a good fattening hog, if he could find one. It was a little early for hog killing, but the fresh meat would not last long enough to spoil and he would smoke a ham for the couple's larder. He would spend the last of his mustering-out pay for his niece. There was little other money in the family.

Lucinda had none and was already trying to sell off her property so she could feed her children in the coming winter, and Elisha had no heart for any celebration. Haley was still sickly, and beginning to be plagued by guilt from the recriminations of her Blackburn family for leaving her husband and children for Elisha. Nor did Elisha have the money he once had, but he gave the couple the cabin on Ripley Knob and supplied a generous supply of whiskey to the wedding guests for his part.

Zachariah and Clarinda could do little; his money had already run out and winter would soon be here. But neither of them, in their shame, could come to the wedding, although their daughter Elizabeth would stand up for Victoria at the ceremony. So when Lum offered to host the affair, there was little other choice and Dorcus gave her assent. There was little joy on Greasy Creek now; it seemed as if a long night had settled in and would not depart. This marriage, she thought, would do much to dispel the darkness that had crept so deeply into everyone's soul.

It was a mark of Dorcus's emerging stature in the family that she was approached to make the decisions. It seemed she was no longer merely Elisha's lieutenant, but had become almost the central authority in the family. At least everyone knew the debt that was owed her. A beautiful young woman who had only been once in love, and at a distance at that, Dorcus had deferred any life of her own for others: the children, the old people, the heartsick wives and lonely sweethearts. She had not once complained to anyone; only the great trees had knowledge of her sorrow and they would not speak.

Making sure the couple got their license was only one of her tasks; she oversaw the preparation of the food, she washed Victoria's wedding dress and stitched its adjustments. She cleaned and prepared the cabin on Ripley Knob for the couple to live with their young daughter. It was the proper place for them to take Rebecca, she thought, since that was where she was conceived, and both Elisha and Joseph had started their marriages there, until children came for either couple and they moved on. Dorcus smiled when she thought that both George and Victoria were probably conceived there as well.

She also persuaded one of the fiddlers on the creek to come to the wedding for a few sprightly tunes, although the prospect of food in that scarce time would probably have been enough of an inducement. On the night before the wedding, she was satisfied that everything had been done that could be done, and the couple would have a proper start in life.

"Now we can wait another day if you're feelin' poorly," she told her cousin while she felt her forehead. "You're still hot, you know."

"I'm just nervous," Victoria replied. "I can't believe it's really happenin'. I just wish Daddy . . . "

"I know, I know," Dorcus reassured her. "But he'll be watchin' and you know that."

On the day of the wedding, Victoria was still flushed, but she stood straight and firm as the preacher struggled through the ceremony. He was an old man who could barely see the book he read from, but had the assistance of an eager young man recently converted to the faith. Robert Damron, formerly of the Thirty-ninth Kentucky, had seen enough of death, and vowed that when he was discharged he would join the church, if it would have him, and spend his life attempting to bind the wounds of the past four years. As the old man recited the words, mostly from memory, Robert gently prompted his lines. In the future, he would perform many marriages and took a special interest and satisfaction when the couples were the children of once-warring soldiers.

After the wedding, Victoria sat down near the fire as plates were taken up and the lines formed around the kitchen table. When everyone had eaten, although Victoria could not take more than a few bites, the music began. The women concluded that her lack of appetite was merely the result of a bride's nervousness, and said nothing more about it, although Victoria barely had the strength to finish a reel with George. Dorcus had ordered the fiddler to play no melancholy tunes, and for the first time in so many years, there was laughter on Greasy Creek, almost a newly returned sense of joy as the last of the guests left Columbus's cabin. In another time, Elisha would have sung the new couple a song or two or three, depending on how much of his whiskey he had partaken, but did not open his mouth this time. Instead he hovered near a still ailing Mahala, who came for a short time to wish the couple well.

The wedding couple departed long before the last of the guests. Dorcus had already some of the boys ahead to light a fire in the cabin and sent some of the girls with them to turn down the bed and sprinkle dried rose petals across it. She had also ordered her charges not to hide in the darkness after completing their mission, but to return immediately and report back to her, which they did, giggling all the while. The petals the girls had strewn, delicate and pale pink, almost white, were the prize of her garden, and as the summer waned she saved them for just this event. The couple took their daughter with them, although Dorcus would have preferred to keep Rebecca with her for the night, since the air was too cold for the baby to be outside unnecessarily. She also knew George and Victoria would have appreciated the privacy, but the baby was still a suckling, and Dorcus had no breast milk to offer her.

Someday I will, she thought. Someday I will too.

After the last of the guests made their good-byes, Dorcus walked back to the farm alone, her path illuminated by the hunter's moon overhead. Before the War, the men and boys of Greasy Creek would have been out in the hills this time of year, after the crops were in, drinking whiskey and smoking pipes or cigars and listening to the hounds chase foxes across the ridges. She knew there was little game these days, but maybe some day it would return and she would hear those sounds again. She smiled as she looked up to Ripley Knob for any light from the cabin, but she could see nothing. That was why George was never found when he deserted. The dense forest kept the light in, but she knew they were there and the night was beautiful in spite of the chill.

It was right, she told herself, that George and Victoria would stay there; there were so many happy memories of that little cabin. Their fathers built it with their own hands when they were barely old enough to slip into the woods by themselves. Both men grew to be men there and made plans for the future while sitting in its doorway. All the Hopkins children had played there. Now two of them would raise their own family there.

But three days after the wedding, Victoria died there.

It may have been the measles that sent George home or it may have been something else he contracted in camp. It may have been any of the diseases they could not combat in those days, made worse by the hunger and privation that weakened everyone, but whatever it was, her fever worsened and her frail body could not fight any longer. At her bedside was her husband and Dorcus, forever her cousin and best friend, and family and friends who watched helplessly as she drifted through the delirium, coming and going until she did not come back. In spite of her grief, only Dorcus had the presence of mind to make arrangements for her funeral.

Elisha forged nails and planed wood for her coffin, and Zachariah helped him construct it, and after the service in Phoebe's cabin, Columbus helped them carry her to the cemetery. George reserved a spot beside her, where he knew he would soon come himself.

Elisha noted that there was little space left in this burying ground, and announced to the family that when the time came for Cornelius and Dorcus, he would bury them where they lived, on the point above the field where only five years ago the family had gathered to celebrate the success of the cotton farm, the same place where Elisha had the awful vision that had now come true.

United by grief, both Confederate and Union veterans, including Zachariah and Columbus, carried her to her rest, just as they had carried so many comrades in so many other places for years. At her grave, there was no longer any animosity for each other, although they silently cursed the War that in its own way had claimed another casualty. If Zachariah hated anyone on that day, it was not the men who had fought against him, but would have been a man who fought beside him. Winright Adkins, who came to the funeral with his family, said nothing, but could feel Zachariah's burning gaze as he listened to the preacher commit Victoria's body to the ground.

With George stunned like a goose hit on the head before the axe fell, there was no one to take care of Rebecca. There were wet nurses on Greasy Creek; Dorcus's sister Bethina had just given birth and was nursing her own child, and Aunt Sally's breasts were still full after her last child, the last child she and Elisha would ever have. But they were afraid for their own children, afraid that whatever had killed Victoria could be passed on, and again it fell to Dorcus to step in. At first, Dorcus made Rebecca a sugar teat with cow's milk and a little honey from the Indians, but Rebecca began to fail with the absence of her mother's breast. She was ill and feverish and a brokenhearted George could not face his child with death apparently so near again.

Like another Hopkins woman in a later lifetime, Dorcus promised the child that she would live, even if she had to suckle her herself, and although she had never borne a child or known a man, she kept that vow. She may have taken medicine from the Indians to bring her dormant breasts to life or she may have simply willed it, but Rebecca Victoria, as she now called her charge, lived and became the first of the children she would raise, hers and others. Before long, Rebecca's inconsolable father gave up beating his head against her grave in his grief, and visited only twice a day, in the morning after he woke up and in the evening before he went to bed. Until he left Greasy Creek with his daughter a decade later, he kept that vigil at her graveside in every kind of weather.

He would often find Clarinda there, visiting her lost children, although her visits were not as frequent since Zachariah sold the farm and rented another one just up the creek. He had no desire to live inside the walls where his youngest daughter had been conceived without him, but he could not hide from the pain even there. With the last of the Mexican gold in his pocket, he left the house, telling Clarinda that he was going to buy food for the family. As he walked by his former home, the bile rose in his throat until he was nearly blinded with rage. Instead of going on to Hamilton's store, Zachariah turned into the yard at Winright Adkins's cabin and demanded that his former comrade sell him corn to grind for his children, since one of them belonged to Winright. But Winright's slammed the door in Zachariah's face, fueling the incendiary rage Zachariah had struggled to contain since he returned. Zachariah smashed his way into the cabin and Winright put a bullet through his heart.

With the nails and wood left over from the coffin he built for Victoria, Elisha built another one for Zachariah, only Clarinda would not have him buried with their children who lay in sight of the cabin where the early memories were forever soiled by the later ones. Instead, she buried him on the hillside above the rented cabin that Zachariah left on the morning of his death, after Dorcus and Clarinda's daughters washed his body and prepared him for the grave, on the same kitchen table where too many men drank from Clarinda's cups. After the funeral, she burned it.

Robert Damron preached his first funeral sermon in that cabin and soldiers from both the Thirty-ninth and the Tenth helped carry Zachariah to his rest. For a brief moment in the troubled years after the War ended, there were no scores to settle after a soldier's funeral, since this tragedy had nothing to do with orders. In time, the owner of the tiny farm, yet another soldier of the Thirty-ninth, gave it to her; a final act of kindness by a soldier who a year before would have followed orders and killed Zachariah himself if the occasion arose.

Winright Adkins, the Confederate comrade and kinsman who killed him, fled after receiving word that Zachariah's brothers were coming for him, combing the hills in rage, and they would not rest until Winright died in a pool of his own blood. Another duty fell to Dorcus, and she went to Elisha and asked him to broker a peace with the brothers, since Winright's own children were now starving and another death would have only added to the misery. Eventually, Winright was allowed to come home to his cabin, where the stain of Zachariah's blood on his kitchen floor never went away.

But there were more deaths for the family, natural and otherwise. In 1867, Samuel Robinson received word from Oklahoma that his first wife had died and he could marry Matilda. He was 73 when they wed and she was 59, and their family was nearly grown. No longer bastard Hopkinses, they assumed the Robinson name and their first chore was to bury their father, who died soon after the wedding, although it was not unexpected. Matilda also reserved a spot near her husband, and when she died in 1880, she became the next to last one buried there, as the family had already begun taking their dead to the flat where Cornelius's cabin stood and where the patriarch and matriarch of the Hopkins clan finally went to their rest. In 1871, Robert Damron formed a church there, which lasted for a hundred years.

In the midst of all the death, a soul came to life on Greasy Creek and it finally sprang from the body of Dorcus herself. It was a son and she named him Harrison for the brother of the man who gave him to her, since her lover already had a wife and children. Harrison was born with a cleft palate, as if he had been marked in compensation for Dorcus's sin, and although Elisha could not have vilified her for the things he had done all his life, he vented his anger on the child.

"You should just let it die," he told her cruelly. "It ain't goin' to live no way."

Dorcus construed that as simply another challenge. It may have been less the child that angered Elisha than it was the fact that Dorcus had become the linchpin of the family in those hard years, but it would

151

not have mattered to her. With the same breasts that fed Rebecca Victoria, Dorcus fed her new son, holding his ruined upper lip together as he nursed and gently tapping his back as her rich milk often slipped through the roof of his mouth and into his lungs.

I do not know if Dorcus looked for someone to seduce in her loneliness or if her lover found her; on that topic Rissie was discreet. But it would be easy to imagine the circumstances of their assignation. For years, Elisha's compound was the center of Greasy Creek; people came and went often, to purchase his liquor or to trade horses and cattle or to buy nails or horseshoes from his forge. It would not be hard to imagine the reaction of a young man who came upon a beautiful young woman with a child at her breast, and after the child was sated, if Dorcus took longer than she should have to cover herself, then that could have prompted a return visit and another and another. Since the young man lived only a few houses away, it would have been easy to make excuses to come back. And after all she had done for others, no one would have denied her some simple happiness, but I suspect the entire family was surprised when her child's eyes kept the blue of his birth long after they should have changed to his mother's dark hue.

They were not Breckinridge's eyes, Dorcus would think to herself, but they were beautiful and kind.

Years later, Dorcus could say with impunity that she had birthed and raised the best man who ever walked on Greasy Creek and no one who knew him would have disagreed. They would not have agreed out of mere sympathy, for there was a certain goodness about Harrison that compensated for his ruined mouth, and that, everyone would agree, was because of the goodness of his mother. What else could have sprung from her womb?

Within only a few years of the War's end, Dorcus had many children to raise and she happily made room for all of them. Both her sisters' marriages failed because both their husbands donned Federal uniforms and fought at Saltville. Neither Elizabeth nor Bethina could forgive them, even though they did not participate in Joseph's capture and were indeed only doing their duty. Dorcus took their youngest children as their mothers gave up on life on Greasy Creek. Haley's children came to Dorcus also, as their mother's vitality waned and their father spent less and less time on Greasy Creek.

With most of the last money he had, Elisha took Haley on a steamboat all the way to Cincinnati to visit a doctor, since the local doctor had pronounced her dying. But the big city doctor only confirmed what Pikeville's doctor had said and Haley came home to make peace with her family on Johns Creek. She tried to make her amends, but the Blackburns still refused to forgive her in spite of her illness, and if she died, they would not welcome her body into the family cemetery. In 1873, Elisha secured a land grant on Grassy Fork of Raccoon Creek, halfway between Greasy Creek and Johns Creek, for her to live out her final days. She would never return to Greasy Creek, and Dorcus moved into Haley's former cabin with her growing brood.

Outside Elisha's compound, the War continued to be fought in Pike County, sometimes in revenge for the victims of wartime crimes, by those who could prove a loss or could buy off a jury, but in many cases scores were settled in pasturelands and lonely country roads. Former soldiers were shot from ambush, houses were burned, and the threat of violence was always in the air. For nearly a decade after Appomattox, there were few families on the Big Sandy that could rest any easier than they could while the country made war on itself and their children made war on each other.

With Elisha gone most of the time, Dorcus persuaded Columbus to move closer to the compound, and from Zachariah's former cabin, he could watch over the family more easily. With the threats he also received, punctuated by the slashed throats of his dogs and pigs, he was grateful for the invitation. Although Dorcus never forgave any soldier of the Thirty-ninth for Joseph's death, she found herself protected by its former soldiers on all sides, but she never noted the irony. She could ignore it because she had more important priorities and they were her children.

For Elisha, who had fought so hard to protect his family on Greasy Creek while the War was raging, his neglect afterward was difficult for the family to understand, but if anyone could see into the man, it would have been Dorcus. She knew what was tearing apart her father: for the first time in his life, he loved someone more than he loved himself, and probably more than life itself.

Elisha had married Phoebe in 1833, when she was not yet twenty and he was not yet eighteen. Dorcus would not have believed that her father never loved her mother, but she knew Elisha, with his great booming voice and magnetic personality, had no problem charming the women. Clans ruled Pike County in its formative years, and the head of the Hopkins clan was Elisha from the time he married. Phoebe never complained when she heard of Elisha's philandering, because it was his prerogative. Neither did she complain when Elisha kept one of his conquests as a second wife a decade later, nor did she complain when he took a third after another decade. But Dorcus sensed even as the War droned on that something was happening to her father, just as something was happening to the last woman he loved. And when he built Haley a cabin for the last days of her life, even Dorcus was not sure he would ever come back.

In spite of the distance from Greasy Creek, Dorcus often made the trek to Grassy, and on each successive visit, she could see the spark fade from Haley's eyes. She could barely find the energy to raise herself as Dorcus washed her hair and bathed her face in cool water. As she had done so many times before for so many others, Dorcus became the mother that Haley had lost in her passion for Elisha. And Dorcus was there the day she died. It was the spring of 1875, a decade after the War had ended, when the hills were finally peaceful again, and birds were singing outside the cabin.

"Won't you sing me . . . a song, Lige?" she asked him. "You never . . . sing anymore."

"I ain't got much of a voice," which broke as he replied. "I'd just call the crows, darlin'."

"Sing me . . ." Her voice was barely a whisper. "Sing me 'Waly, Waly.' That was always . . . always my favorite." Her breath was coming in short gasps now; her eyes were clouding, and Elisha could not think of a way to grant her request.

"Please . . ." she asked him again. "You sung it to me . . . the first time you met me."

Dorcus could see the shudders racking his great body as he struggled to find the strength. He opened his mouth once and failed to speak, but then by some force that awed even his daughter, something came over him and he summoned the voice that had fled from him years ago and softly mouthed the words:

The water is wide, I can't cross o'er,
Nor do I have bright wings to fly,
Give us a boat, which can carry two,
And both shall row, my love and I.

He sang the verse and stopped; only one verse, but he knew she did not have time for another. Yet it made her smile as her eyes lit up for the last time.

"But we . . . don't have . . . bright wings . . . do we, Lige?" she asked, and then she was gone.

Leaves

*I*impatiently *tapped my fingers on the countertop as I waited for the clerk in the Kentucky State Archives to retrieve the documents I had ordered. She had passed my request through a dumbwaiter to the upstairs storage area a few minutes before and told me that the documents would come back in a small basket and she would let me know when they arrived. I sat down and watched the second hand move on the wall clock as I waited. I made doodles on the yellow pad I had brought with me. I occasionally glanced through the windows at the fall evening outside the building. Autumn had closed in unexpectedly. As I drove down to Frankfort that afternoon, waves of brown and gold leaves had skittered across the pavement in the bright sunlight. It would be cold soon, I thought; another winter was on its way.*

The previous spring, we had wrapped up work on the cemeteries and moved all the graves we could find to a place where they would be safe. I had dutifully recounted the stories I could tell in a book about my family and thought this chapter of my life was completed. I thought I had found all I could find about Elisha Hopkins, about the Old Ones, about the lives once led on Greasy Creek, but here I was researching again, nervously awaiting another scrap of information about the past.

When I heard the small elevator door open, I nearly leaped from my chair to see if the basket held what I was looking for. The clerk smiled when she confirmed it was my request and handed it to me; I think she could sense how desperately I wanted the dusty papers that had been untouched for nearly a century.

"Thank you, ma'am," I said, attempting to be courteous and restrain my excitement as I whisked the basket from her hands. This

was my second visit to the Archives, and there was considerably more urgency this time.

Since my first trip, something had been troubling me. For months now, I had anguished over what seemed to be an inaccuracy in one of Rissie's stories. She said that Elisha had died on Ripley Knob, where he was living and where he now rests, but my information indicated she was wrong. I had studied the census records and found that in 1900 he was living with his last family beside George W. Blackburn, his second son by Haley, up Main Greasy Creek and quite a distance away from the mountaintop. By the 1910 census, Elisha was gone, and his weathered sandstone marker was still readable. The date said July 1904. Four years before, he was living up main Greasy Creek. I could understand his family taking him back to Ripley to be buried, but Rissie said he was living there when he died.

In addition to the mystery of his last years, I could find nothing of Mary, his last wife, legal or otherwise, after his death. Their three sons, Will, Paris, and Hooker, were living with Harrison Hopkins and his family in 1910, but I could find no trace of Mary in any census. She was still a relatively young woman at the turn of the century, so she should have been living somewhere in 1910. I thought she may have moved with one of her sons to another county, but I could find no trace of her there either. What had become of her?

I thought it odd that Rissie had never told me anything about Mary; I had gleaned everything I knew about her from my own research. Why had I been told nothing of the only wife of Elisha Hopkins that Rissie might actually have known? But that question was peripheral to the reason I had come to Frankfort. Rissie said Elisha had died in the cabin where he lived, but the evidence said otherwise. Although such a discrepancy would be a minor point, an inconsequential detail for most family histories, I was obsessed with finding the truth. It was part of my penance that I had become so meticulous, after decades of being anything but. I had become a partisan of my grandmother's stories; I had found not one, not one, that was contrary to the facts I later accumulated, and I would brook no suggestion that she could have been mistaken.

I knew that Rissie's stories about the Old Ones were actually Dorcus's stories, since Rissie was born in April of 1904 and Elisha died the following July. Rissie would have had no personal memory of him or of anyone who died before she was born, so a small inconsistency would have to be forgiven. Yet her stories were clear and authoritative, as if she had been there. That was obviously due to Dorcus's faithful recounting, and Rissie's dutiful preservation, but something was still missing from the family narrative. It was like I had walked into a room in which the furniture had been subtly rearranged and I could not detect what was different.

On the yellow pad I had brought to the Archives to take notes, I once again put Rissie's stories in the order in which they happened and I could again see the hiatus, the gap in the family chronology. The very last years were missing from the timeline. Although a great deal of what she had told me was forever lost, I still remembered enough and had recovered enough to tell much of the Hopkins family history. But between 1900 and Elisha's death in 1904, I could not recall a sliver of anything that Rissie had told me. Admittedly, I had been careless and squandered too many of her gifts, but I somehow felt this was not my fault.

On this seemingly trivial issue, my ghosts had suddenly become reticent. It once startled me at how rapidly the memories came tumbling back when I asked for their help. As I wrote my first book, it seemed all of them were taking turns looking over my shoulder, as if they were telling me to change a word here, a phrase there. But they would not speak of the years after the old century ended. No one spoke when I broached this subject. I could no longer conjure those gentle spirits who were once so willing to tell me who I was and where I came from.

Are you all hiding something from me, I began to wonder? Is the reason I can remember nothing because I was told nothing? Had Rissie deliberately kept something from me, or had Dorcus kept something from her?

Sometimes answers come when one least expects them, and sometimes for questions not yet asked. When I came across a reference to an old court case from Pike County that had gone to the Kentucky Court of Appeals and it mentioned Elisha's name, I felt an almost electric shock. Only the bare facts were presented in the summary, so I determined to look at the entire case file. Could I find some clue there about his last days that would settle all this for me? I hoped so.

I almost didn't go.

Initially, I wasn't sure I wanted to find the truth. I did not want to find anything that would disprove Rissie. It wasn't just that I had published a book and did not want to find that I had been wrong about something. I had spent too much of my life denying her and I was now fiercely protective of her memory. Of course, I was twenty years too late to thank her, I reminded myself again, a little abashed that I was once more seeking proof before I believed her. But I went anyway, because the possibility of learning what happened to Elisha in his last years was too much to resist.

Now here I was with what I knew would settle the matter, even before I opened the file, and I was almost afraid to look at it.

With no small amount of trepidation, I began reading and slowly turned the pages of the yellowed, faded documents. They were as lifeless and brittle as the leaves that had swarmed across my path as I drove down that afternoon. I wondered again if I should have made this trip or if I should even be opening this file, but here I was and now I would find out why I came.

I began reading and found myself taking shallow breaths; almost afraid to take in air for fear that whatever truth I was seeking would fly away if I exhaled.

I took notes as I read. I took clearer notes when I realized I could not read my own jagged handwriting.

I read slowly and carefully. When I finished reading, I placed the file in order, straightened the pages, and read it again, taking more notes. I gave it one final read before I looked up at the clock on the wall. The archivist cleared her throat; it was closing time. I had been reading and writing for an hour and did not realize I had been so engrossed.

Finally I slumped back in my chair and let go the breath I had been holding.

Jesus Christ, I thought, no wonder they kept this from me.

Chapter Seven

After the Fall

Steamboat traffic resumed on the Big Sandy after the War, but in truth it had never really stopped. Publication of schedules had ceased because of the threat of attacks by outlaw gangs when the boats made port, but merchants always knew when the smokestacks could be seen rounding bends at Pikeville or Prestonsburg or Paintsville, the three P's of towns on the upper Big Sandy.

For years after hostilities ended, overland routes remained dangerous, and steamboat lines capitalized on the safety of river shipping. Merchandise filled the holds and covered the decks when steamers went either way. New gingham or quinine or coffee grinders went upstream and hogs and hemp bales came back down. Later on, after sawmills appeared, downstream boats carried sawn lumber bound for Cincinnati or Louisville, although they had to lay over occasionally to avoid the annual flood of logs from the timber companies who sent out their product in any way they could.

After the War, boat captains noted the absence of certain of their regular wartime passengers, although passenger traffic increased when hostilities ended, and some boats even added calliopes for their discerning customers. The passengers who did not return no longer had business in the hills, although they had never spoken of what they did when they were regulars. Some said they were spies, both Union and Confederate agents regularly playing cards in the captain's quarters. It was said there was an unspoken agreement between the two sides that neither would take action against the other, since the lines of communication either way were too valuable to be lost. The Big Sandy was a direct link to Louisville, which was Union headquarters in the West, and to the Confederate lines on the edge of Pike County, where secret agents slipped through the mountain passes almost at will. When the War ended, many of the men who learned their poker faces on the tiny Big Sandy steamers applied them with much success on the big riverboats of the Mississippi when service resumed to New Orleans.

Cotton from Pike County, however, was never shipped out again.

Among the new surge of passengers were evangelists, reflecting a new appreciation of the church for the mountaineers. There had been so much death, so many young souls lost prematurely during the War, before they could get right with the Lord, that their families had not been able to say good-bye. Fervent prayers went up for admission of the lost into heaven, and an increase in tombstones was noted in postwar manifests, although much of the finely cut marble had cost its recipients the last reserves of cash they had. The greater portion of Pike County families, however, remembered their dead as they always did: with a flat creek rock that they would take to a scribe to chisel names of the departed onto it.

Elisha wanted to buy Haley a grand stone, but he no longer had the money, and it was doubtful her family would have let him erect it, even though it would not have taken up space in their family cemetery. The Blackburn women had refused to allow her to be buried with the rest of the Blackburn dead. If her brother had not given Elisha a gravesite on a hill across from the Blackburn cemetery, he would have taken her back to Greasy Creek, which was what he wanted to do, but he abided by her last wish: that she would rest forever near her father and mother, a daughter's atonement for what she did when she left her first family for her second.

There was much unsaid after the War; Mammy described those years as much like the aftermath of a great tree falling: when it crashed to the ground the air was pushed out and became deadly silent, like the eye of a tornado. At times it seemed that even the crows were too frightened to speak, although only crows sang Haley's funeral dirge the day she died. For Elisha, the silence continued long afterward.

For a year after her death, he was numb; he could feel nothing and wanted to feel nothing, so he turned to drink. In his lifetime, he had sold enough whiskey to float any steamboat that came up the Big

Sandy, but used little of his production himself, at least no more than any other mountaineer. He had been rich enough to easily support three families with no stigma attached to his work.

Before the War, drinking was common, but generally thought of, at least by men, as a blessing, a joy, something nature provided to accentuate life's pleasures, as well as a lubricant for the tongue of many a reluctant singer. Women used it as medication to dull the pain of childbirth, to help reduce a fever, or to fight off a chill. Mixed with a little turpentine and sugar, it was given to children every spring as a preventative for worms. Only a few used it as a way to escape life's tragedies.

But after the War, there was little joy and too many tragedies, and whiskey was even more in demand, too much in demand and too frequently used, especially by men whose memories of the ugly years frequently boiled over into pointless violence. The emotional injuries of the Civil War had never healed and would never fully heal. It took little to bring them back ferociously, especially if alcohol eased their passage. Zachariah was not the only soldier to escape death during the War, only to return home and die at the hand of a former friend. The faintest slight between men could provoke deadly confrontations. Old animosities often flared anew at unsuspecting times, prompting drunken veterans to launch new attacks against their former rivals, even if their rivals were dead. Besotted veterans would sometimes go into cemeteries where rivals were buried, dig up their rotting corpses and roll them into nearby roads, leaving macerated limbs in their wake.

Such outrages would prompt retaliation, and more violence, extending the hatred through generations. Many mountain feuds were directly traceable to a war that was long over. For many years, the hills were lawless, especially in Eastern Kentucky, which did not have Federal soldiers enforcing Reconstruction as in neighboring Virginia. Although the harsh bootheel of Union occupation was unwelcome in Virginia, it prevented much of the savagery that was so common just across the border in Kentucky or in the upstart state of West Virginia.

Saloons cropped up overnight, and what little money mountaineers could make was often squandered at makeshift bars and poker games that lasted for days. In that regard, Greasy Creek not much different from the rest of the country: drunken Civil War veterans were largely responsible for Carrie Nation's first rampage with a hatchet in 1900.

In the midst of such a whiskey boom, Elisha could have become wealthy again, but he was no longer a successful purveyor of spirits. When Haley took ill, he began to drink more and sell less, until he sold almost none at all, although he occasionally returned to Greasy Creek to fire up his still. But on those trips, he would stay alone at the cabin on Ripley Knob, avoiding his own families, and returning alone to the empty cabin he built for Haley on Grassy Creek.

He no longer wanted anything to do with his three families on Greasy Creek. Phoebe's children were all grown, already parents, along with Sally's, except for Harmon, who was thirteen years old when he lost his father as assuredly as his father had lost Aunt Haley. It was not an easy thing for a boy approaching manhood to accept, and Harmon Robinson never completely forgave his father for abandoning him.

"Why won't Poppy speak to me anymore?" Harmon would ask his mother, but she had no reply. Indeed Elisha had stopped speaking to her as well. When Haley wanted to move closer to her family, the family that still rejected her, Elisha forsook all his other families for her, living only for her until she died. Sally began to teach Harmon what her family had taught her. She was of the People, and she knew things, things that her son would need: how to be fend for himself, how to draw strength from the trees and the mountains, how to use certain powers she had been given and neglected while she still had Elisha. Of all their children, Harmon was the only son and he looked like all of Elisha's sons. Whether they were Hopkins, Blackburn or Robinson, Elisha's features could be seen in all of them, the bold forehead, the shock of black hair, and the piercing eyes. But although they were recognizably his sons, he ultimately abandoned them all. Sally did not know if Elisha would ever return or if he would make up with Harmon if he did, but she knew a son needed a legacy, even if it did not come from his father, so she gave him what she could of herself.

Greasy Creek once was rife with tales of Harmon's abilities; how he could call animals from the woods, how he could make chairs walk, how he put a curse on a neighbor's corn mill and lifted it when the neighbor offered a bottle of whiskey in compensation for the slight that brought the spell down on him. Sally taught those things to none of her other children, but she did not need to; until they were grown, all her other children had a father to care for them. When Haley died, most of Elisha died too.

After her death, Haley's children moved in with Dorcus, who kept her promise and had already taken on the responsibility of guiding two fatherless families through post-Civil War Pike County. Both Joseph and Zack's families needed her, and she no longer considered it unfair to take on that responsibility. Her first attempt at love gave her Harrison with his cleft palate, and then later another son whose lips were whole. She named him Joseph in honor of her dead uncle so that he would remember his namesake and his family and keep the memories alive.

"You got to tell the stories some day, baby," she would tell him as he grew up. "You know how hard it is for your brother to talk."

Joseph faithfully promised her that he would. He knew he had to; although Harrison would have told the stories if he could, the rest of the family wanted no part of the past.

Her sisters Elizabeth and Bethina divorced their husbands after the War had thrown insurmountable obstacles to their marriages, and their youngest children came to Dorcus as well. She made room for them in her home, welcoming them and giving them the love their warring parents had run out of. Dorcus no longer chafed at her bonds, because she knew that was not what they were, and she accepted the role life had given her.

And she was no longer Dorcus, or Belle; she was now "Mammy," and that was what she would be called for the rest of her life. She wore her bonnets, like most of the matrons of Greasy Creek, but they were always brightly colored. She wanted her children to remember nothing grim about her, although she took the role of mother seriously. She had loved no man for years, and having a man in her life was no longer important; only her children meant anything to her, and she had many, whether she had birthed them or not.

She had found her calling.

She was Mammy; she would be Mammy forever, and eventually all of Greasy Creek called her that.

Belle, the young girl who dreamed of a famous man with ice-blue eyes, a man to whom she gave an embroidered pillow, was gone. When word came of Breckinridge's death in 1875, the youthful Belle had already died an unnoticed death. Dorcus was gone as well; the grandmother she was named for was in her grave, and the dutiful granddaughter's heart slept under the older Dorcus's breast. Now only Mammy remained; and she was satisfied.

In 1877, Phoebe filed for divorce from Elisha. In the lawsuit, she cited abandonment; and the facts were indisputable. Elisha would not come home from the cabin he had built for Haley on Grassy Creek and would not support Phoebe, his only legal wife. If he came to Greasy Creek at all, it was to make another run of whiskey, his presence announced only by the smoke coming from his still. He would not pause to visit his families and gave them no money to live on, although like most people of the hills after the War, he had little to give.

The court agreed that Elisha had abandoned Phoebe and granted her divorce. Her lawsuit was intended to be more of a wake-up call to Elisha than a serious effort to terminate their marriage, but he did not contest it or even acknowledge it. When the sheriff delivered his summons, he used it to light a fire on the hearth.

Phoebe was surprised at how swiftly her marriage had been dissolved, since lawsuits caused by the War were still clogging the court system in Pike County in spite of a state law that was intended to quash them. But even after she was free of Elisha, she was no better off than before. She was seventy-two years old, and depended on her children for support.

She had no choice but to call on her daughter to intercede, and like all the other requests she been given throughout her life, Mammy tried her best to honor it.

On a cold spring day, when the redbuds were blooming in spite of the chill, a buckboard made its way up the serpentine Grassy Creek road. It stopped near a forlorn cabin that looked unoccupied, except for the thin wisp of smoke emanating from the rock chimney and a half-opened door that slammed shut as the buckboard neared it. Perhaps for lack of a working latch, the door creaked open again and Mammy got down from the wagon and approached it. Waiting in the wagon were John Miles Hopkins, Joseph's only son, and Joseph Phillips, Zachariah Phillips's second oldest son, the one his parents had named for Elisha's Confederate brother.

"Lige," she called to him through the open doorway of the cabin. "Lige, are you in there?" She heard no response.

"Daddy, are you in there?" she repeated, and this time she heard movement, but no one answered the door.

"It's Belle," she said, reverting to the name he gave her when he determined Dorcus was not a sprightly enough name for his beautiful child. "Daddy, I'm comin' in."

Elisha looked at her through red-rimmed eyes as she pushed open the door and walked in. He was sitting at a sagging table with a bottle and a cup in front of him. She could see no food as she briefly surveyed the room, wondering when was the last time he had eaten, and opened her mouth to speak when he cut her off.

"How you been, Sister?" he said in a husky voice as she closed the door against the cool spring air.

"I been doin' very well, Daddy," she said as she came over to where he was sitting. There was one other chair at the table and she sat in it.

"What do you want?" he asked, glaring at her.

"I want you to come home with me," she said. "Mother needs you, Pap."

"Needs me?" he exploded. "God damn it girl, she divorced me."

"We all need you," she said quietly. "It ain't the same on Greasy Creek without you."

"It ain't the same on Greasy Creek with or without me," he said reflectively.

"There's somethin' else, Daddy," she said. "Uncle Joe's children want to go visit his grave and they asked me to take them."

Elisha's bloodshot eyes widened when he heard her words. Children? Joe's children? He thought of his own sons and daughters, and unexpected waves of guilt washed over him. Where are my children? He could not remember when he had last seen them. How long had it been? He had not wanted to see his children by Phoebe and Sally because they were not Haley's, and he had not wanted to see Haley's because they were. He thought he needed no reminders of what he had lost.

But with the guilt came realization that he was not the only one to have lost, and he shut his red-streaked eyes, waiting for her to continue.

166

"I don't know the way to Joe's grave, Daddy, and you do. You went there once, with some men, but the children want to go before it's too late."

Elisha opened his eyes as Mammy spoke, and to her relief his glare softened; he remembered the search for his brother's grave. He had made the trip not long after the War ended. He wanted to make sure Joseph had a proper grave, or bring his body back if he had not been honorably buried, and he found it in a peaceful cemetery behind the church where his funeral was preached. Joseph lay beside the two other men who had fallen with him that day, in a plot owned by a fine gentleman, a doctor who had once served under Breckinridge himself.

"It's a right pretty place," he said. "I was goin' to bring him home, but I didn't know which grave was his. There are three stones . . ."

"I remember, Daddy," she softly interjected. "You told me. But his children want to see it anyway."

Elisha reached for his cup and lifted it almost to his lips, but then put it back on the table. He stared at it for a moment and then got up and flung what was in it into the fire. Evanescent flames shot up from the desultory embers that lay dying on the hearth.

"When do they want to go?" he asked her.

"As soon as you're ready," she replied. "They asked me to ask you if you would go with them."

"It'd be dangerous for them to go alone," he said. "Bandits, rogues everywhere."

He paused and looked out the smoke-covered windows of the cabin before he spoke again. "I guess I could take them."

"I've got John Miles and Joe Phillips out in the wagon," she told him. "If you want to, they'll help you load up here."

Elisha looked around the nearly barren cabin and sighed; many of the household items he had accumulated with Haley were gone already. Some he had given to needy families on Grassy and some had been stolen while he was away, and he had replaced nothing. He wanted nothing, since the only thing he wanted he could not have.

"There ain't much here," he said with a long sigh. He had waited for Haley to come back, even as a ghost. He had gotten drunk enough at times to make himself believe that she was with him in the room, but had come to his senses when he sobered up. A few times he thought he had felt her hair move across his face as he slept and immediately awoke to call her name, but he never heard a response.

"John Miles is out there?" he asked her.

"Yes, sir," she replied.

"And Little Joe?"

"Yes, sir. He's all growed up, but still little," she said with a faint smile.

"Is Clary doin' all right?" he asked.

"Yes, sir," she said. "Adelaide stays with me a right smart, but Clary's doin' very well." Elisha knew the vernacular. "Very well" meant only passable in the language of the hills, but it was as much as could be expected in these times.

Dorcus watched his chest rise and fall under his dirty shirt and his head drifted downward to his chest, but she knew he was not sleeping. He was deep in thought, making his good-byes to this cabin and to the ghost that would not haunt it. He did not speak until he raised his head and looked at his daughter, the one person in his life most truly his heir.

"I guess it's time to go home," he said, as he wiped his bloodshot eyes.

He collected only a few things from the cabin and went out into the chilly spring air with his daughter and climbed into the buckboard. The boys sat in the back, fearful of speaking to the man they remembered more as a god than a mere mortal. When they drove away, Mammy did not recall him looking back at the cabin that he left for the last time in his life.

"Look at the redbuds," she told him as they bounced their way down the creek. "Ain't they pretty?"

The sun broke through the clouds as she spoke, warming them with feeble light, but with the promise of brighter days, and birds were already in song.

"I forgot it was spring," Elisha said.

A few days later, the sun had strengthened when a party on horseback left Pike County, bound for the crossroads town of Bloomfield in Nelson County, in the Bluegrass, far away from the mountains. They traveled over the same road Breckinridge had taken flight over in 1861, and the same road Burbridge had brought his army across in 1864, returning with Joseph as a prisoner. All of Joseph's children, except for Victoria, and most of their spouses were in the group with Mammy tending to all of them, as if they were mere children again.

Mammy had left her young charges in the care of Adelaide Phillips, who was thrilled with the responsibility and happy to return the many favors Mammy had done for her family. Now thirteen, she was growing up rapidly, and often sat in rapt attention as Mammy told her about her father, whom she was not even sure she remembered. Mammy was determined that Adelaide would keep Zachariah's memory alive, and until she died, Adelaide would proudly tell anyone she met that her daddy was with the president when the War ended. Everyone knew which president he was.

Joseph's widow was not with her family on the trip; Elisha told Lucinda before what he had found on his first trip and she was no more able to make the journey now than she was then, although she might have gone if she could have known for sure which grave was her husband's. But she stayed at home and waited for young Joe Phillips and his sister to make their daily trips across Little Creek to make sure she was safe.

The Hopkins party stopped to camp at spots along the way to Bloomfield, and Elisha began to share stories of his brother with his family, some stories that he had told before, and many he thought that he had forgotten. He was surprised that the stories came back so easily as he told them, and he even sang a ballad that he and his brother had sung when they played together on Ripley Knob. It was an old English tune that Cornelius had taught them, and they sang it when they cut the trees and dressed the logs they rolled into place for their cabin.

As Elisha began to recite a tale, he would look around the campfire at their faces, faces no longer of children, and he was again reminded that he had none of his own anymore, except for Harmon, and he realized that he had probably lost him. He had grandchildren, of course, but for whatever reason, pride or the folly of a man fighting against time, he suddenly yearned for children again, his own children, and the thought crossed his mind that he might just start a new family when he returned.

When they arrived in Bloomfield, Elisha led them to a cemetery on a hill and to a plot where ornately carved stones dominated the grassy space within it. To the left of the plot, three finely cut stones sat in precise order, three stones with no caption on them whatsoever. When Elisha had come before, there were only rocks to mark their graves, but these new stones revealed no more information than before.

"Which one is Daddy's?" America asked, turning to her Uncle Lige with the question.

"We don't know, child," he replied. "I asked everybody I could when I come here before, but no one knew." The new stones were also unmarked. "Looks like they still don't"

"Which one do we decorate?" she asked, holding a handful of crepe-paper flowers that they had made from purchases in Lexington when they passed through there. Elisha had appropriated some of them to place on Breckinridge's grave when they stopped there on the way to Bloomfield. He knew Belle would want to visit that place, too. In addition to the artificial flowers, she had brought three flowering plants from her garden with them, since Elisha had already told her that he did not know which grave was Joseph's.

"We decorate all of them," Mammy said as she began pulling weeds around the blank markers. "All of them deserve it."

Before they left Bloomfield, Elisha discreetly asked the Joshua Gore family, who owned the plot, if any new information had been found as to which Confederate soldier had been buried where, but although the family had purchased the stones and erected them in honor of the soldiers, no one knew which was which. Indeed, even the man who preached their funerals was not sure of their names. The Union Army had left their bodies in the road after the execution, and few of the people who witnessed it could remember much of what the sergeant said when he read their death warrants. Even if they had known, they might not have carved their names on the stones, since tensions were still high from the War, especially in Bloomfield, which still suffered from its support of the Confederacy, and no one wanted to risk desecration of the graves of three soldiers of the Cause. Dr. Gore himself, who had served under Breckinridge in the Orphan Brigade as brigade surgeon, had taken a chance by allowing the boys to be buried there. Union partisans could have destroyed his own family stones, but no damage had been done and he ordered the erection of proper stones after the War, except there were no names to carve onto them. Bloomfield seemed to value its heritage, and although Elisha left again without the body of his brother, he was satisfied. He knew his brother's grave would be tended forever.

Spring had come earlier to Bloomfield that it had to the mountains, and wildflowers gave truth to the name of the village. The hilltop cemetery was a pretty place and it looked over the Baptist church where a Methodist minister preached the funeral of Joseph and his companions, since the Baptist preacher had been penalized before and was fearful of more retaliation. But the War was over, and Joseph's family was pleased. Comforted that all had been done that could be done, they said their final good-byes and began their long journey back to Pike County.

"Did Daddy die near here?" one of the girls asked him, and Elisha was almost unable to reply. He had been to the place where his brother was shot, but he did not want to take the children. It was just a few miles away on the Bardstown road, but Elisha professed ignorance.

"Somewhere near here, Sissy," he said. "But I 'spect we'd better be on our way home." They don't need to see that, he thought. This place is all they need to remember.

When they returned to Pike County, Elisha moved into the Ripley Knob cabin and restarted his whiskey-making business to immediate success. His Indian friends gladly supplied him once more with honey for his product and he rarely had to leave his mountaintop to deliver it. A steady stream of customers made it unnecessary. At the same time, he began his search for another bride, eventually finding one who, like Haley, was married to someone else at the time. But that was a minor detail for Elisha and it took little to woo her from her husband, perhaps too little, as he may have later determined.

Mary Riley married her distant cousin John Riley in Russell County, Virginia after he had served a year in a Confederate regiment, and together they came to Kentucky. They came to escape the War, but he later joined the Thirty-ninth Kentucky and was at the Saltville fight where Joseph was captured, acting as scout for the Union Army. He knew the mountains of Southwest Virginia well, although he planned never to return to them. He planned to stay in his adopted county until he died, but without the order imposed by Federal troops deployed in the Reconstruction of Virginia, Pike County was no safer after the War than it was during it, maybe less. Thieves and marauders who had hidden behind the cloak of partisan activity during the War continued to prey on the innocent after the last surrender. John Riley moved back to Russell County. His wife was expecting again, and he would not take a chance on his daughter entering the world fatherless. He expected to find a piece of land and live quietly, but even though the roads were safe because of the omnipresent army patrols, he quickly discovered that he could not come home again. He could not find work, his life was threatened for his Union service, and he was shunned by nearly everyone he knew. The family that remained could not forgive him for going over to the enemy, and after Mary recovered from the birth, he reluctantly made his way back to Pike County. Better to die as a man, he thought, than to live with the reputation of a coward. At least he could live among comrades in Pike, although some of them remembered the War largely through a haze of alcohol. By the time the century ended, his family in Virginia had forgiven him and he had mostly forgiven himself, although he never forgave Mary for what she did.

Elisha met Mary when he made a rare delivery of a load of whiskey to a cheaply built shack that served as a saloon on Caney Creek, the next hollow up Shelby Creek, just above where Lucinda lived on the remnant of the cotton farm. The Rileys lived near the saloon, and Mary would cook the irregular meals the proprietor served, while John, like so many former soldiers, attempted to piece together a life of farming and logging. Mary was friendly to Elisha and was flattered that he took time to speak to her. His reputation, both for his whiskey and for his way with women, had preceded him. She would have a meal ready for him on the days he made his deliveries. He was equally flattered at the attention she gave him. It was not long before he would stay late at the saloon while his Indian friends stayed outside in the buckboard, napping when they were not grinning or shaking their heads.

Before long, Mary went to Ripley Knob with Elisha. He may have taken a perverse pleasure in taking the wife of former Union soldier John Riley, who served with Ezekiel Prater and Elisha's Union brother Columbus, or the thought may never have crossed his mind, but John did not challenge him. He was not the first man who had lost a woman to Elisha Hopkins, and he knew that to fight him might only have only gotten him killed. Men were dying from less in Pike County. He may have also had his reservations about how faithful Mary had been to him, and he went back to Russell County once more and divorced her. But he had other children to raise, and he eventually came again to Pike to find a new wife, since the Virginia girls would not have him.

The youngest child of John and Mary was an infant daughter too young for Mary to leave behind, and Mary made only one demand on Elisha: that she would take that daughter with her to Greasy Creek. Her name was Delilafare, and it was to both Elisha and Mary's credit (and Mammy's demand) that they allowed John to continue to see her as she grew up. Elisha treated her no differently than he had treated any of his daughters, but he wanted sons. Elisha married Mary in 1879 and before long the new arrivals began. He was sixty-four years old when he wed for the last time, but to prove he was still the strong Elisha of old, he led his team alone as he hauled a new cast-iron stove up the hill to the cabin on Ripley Knob, enlarged now for his new family. Almost at his bidding, Mary had no more daughters and presented him with three sons.

For a while, he was reasonably happy, and he even allowed Phoebe to move in with them. There was nothing sexual in his relationship with his divorced first wife, but she needed a home, and Mammy arrived with her one day and simply ordered her father to take in her mother. Elisha told the census taker in 1880 that she was his "widowed sister," and slapped his knees in laughter as the man departed. He still enjoyed a joke, although the occasions for his laughter were few.

Although Mammy was an infrequent visitor to the Ripley Knob cabin, she and her father frequently argued about his treatment of Harrison. He accepted her son Joe, who was a handsome boy with perfect features, and he even stood up for him when Joe was married at Mammy's house, but there was a special cruelty he extended to Harrison because of his harelip.

"You can't believe how mean Ol' Lige was to Daddy," Rissie would say. "He never had a good word for him until he died."

I do not know why Elisha vented his wrath on Harrison so many times; other people told me how mean he had been, and they could not understand either, but I suspect it had something to do with the War.

So many strong, handsome boys had gone away, only to return crippled in mind or body, or had not returned at all, their graves lost, covered over by the grass of distant fields. Elisha valued sons and always preferred the company of men. Perhaps he thought that Harrison, because of his defect, was somehow not fit to be included in the pantheon of heroes he had known. Whatever the case, it infuriated him even more when Harrison married Delilafare.

Mammy had taken her away from Elisha and Mary before their last son was born. She called her "Lila," as would everyone who knew her and the young girl looked forward to the nights she could stay with Mammy because her home was bright and happy and full of children. By contrast, Elisha's home seemed to be cloaked in gloom as he grew older and the fact that Mary was still a relatively young woman began to weigh on him. Eventually Harrison and Lila fell in love. In 1889 they married and began their own lives together. Elisha did not attend the wedding, although Mary did, and she brought some of Elisha's whiskey with her for the celebration. She also drank a large portion of it herself, and flirted with some of the men in attendance.

As Elisha's sons grew up, they called Harrison "Uncle," although he was actually their brother-in-law or nephew, depending on how one attempted to sort out the family lineage. With Elisha's many wives, it was never an easy task. He now had four families, and perhaps even he forgot some of his children by the time he died.

The two constants in Elisha's life were his whiskey and his friendship with the Indians. The trappings of society never appealed to him, and the loyalty of his Indian friends was never in doubt. Every year, he would take the honey they brought him and concoct the most unique brew Pike County had ever tasted, and until he became too old to produce it, he was happiest minding his still.

With Haley gone, he took only a perfunctory interest in family life, although Will, his first son by Mary, was close to his father. Elisha named him for Wilburn Blackburn, "Monkey Will," Haley's brother, the one who had defied his family to give her a final resting place to the consternation of the Blackburn women. Elisha sometimes took young Will with him when he visited the Indians and stayed up all night around their campfires, drinking and telling stories, although Will would often fall into the lap of one of the Indian women long before the men gave up their reveries. There were fewer men around the fires on those nights, unlike the way it was before the War came, when chants from a dozen voices could be heard up and down Greasy Creek. Some of the Indian boys had not come home either, and Elisha had joined his friends more than once in their funeral songs.

One cool fall day, while Elisha was working at his still under a cliff just beyond the cabin, he heard a horse slowly clopping its way up the mountain road. Although he could not see through the trees, he heard a familiar voice speaking to Phoebe and then heard the horse make its way toward him. Presently, Winright Adkins came into view. It had been a long time since his nephew visited him, although at one time Winright had been one of Elisha's best customers.

Since Elisha had saved him from Zack's brothers, after Mammy had interceded with her father, Winright had stayed out of trouble, and although he still drank, he was not known for his belligerent drunkenness. But that was the same drunkenness that marked so many of the former soldiers, especially Confederate soldiers, as they tried to adapt to a life that no longer appreciated warriors, especially warriors of a lost cause. From his horse, Winright looked closely at the great figure that straightened slightly as he approached.

After all these years, Lige ain't changed much, he thought. He was broke awful bad when that woman died, but he's still makin' that shine. He don't much look like he did when he could whip the devil with one hand and grab a pretty woman with the other.

But Elisha still exuded power. Winright wondered if it was that power or his whiskey that made him so attractive to women. He noted to himself that Elisha was on his fourth family and was still having children.

That old man can still cut the mustard, he thought. All those girls wouldn't have stayed with him if it was just whiskey.

Winright offered a friendly salutation to Elisha and got off his horse to walk toward him. Elisha could see the hog leg pistol under Winright's coat, the pistol he always carried at his side, the same pistol he had carried during the War and had used so tragically afterward. Elisha carried no weapon anymore, although most men did. The violence had finally slowed, although Greasy Creek had never and would never return to the peace that once marked its existence. Almost daily, families announced they were leaving, no longer able to deal with the Greasy Creek they now hated and the memories that haunted them. From his vantage point high on the mountaintop, Elisha saw no reason to venture into the valley below, and even when he did, he went unarmed. He had long ago determined he would not raise a weapon again.

"Smells good, Lige," he said. "You wouldn't let a man have a little taste of that, would you?"

"Surely," Elisha said. He picked up one of the earthen casks and handed it to him. "This is the first one," he said. "It just came through the strainer. Ought to be cool by now."

Winright took a small sip and then a larger one.

"God damn, that's good," he said.

"What brings you up here, Winright?" Elisha asked, knowing that his visitor would not have made the trek up Ripley Knob without a reason.

"Lige, I just wanted ask you somethin'," he began. "I kindly wish you'd talk to Belle for me."

"Talk to Belle?" Elisha asked. "She's a grown woman with two children. What in hell you want me to talk to her about?"

"Well, I took Adelaide a new dress and gave it to Clary and no sooner than I got home, here comes Belle and throws it back in my face."

Elisha said nothing, and waited for Winright to continue.

"Lordy, she was mad," Winright laughed. "She said if I ever brought that girl anything else she'd kill me."

"So?" Elisha asked him. "What business is that of mine?"

"Hell, Lige, I just wanted to give her somethin'. After all, I am her daddy."

Elisha stared at him for a long moment, his brow knitting gravely before he replied.

"No, you ain't," he said deliberately. "You killed her daddy."

"God damn it, Lige," Winright replied quickly. "You know I didn't have no choice."

"I know that, but Adelaide's a Phillips, not an Adkins. If I was you, I'd pay attention to Belle. You ought to know the way she is."

"But I just wanted to give Adelaide a little somethin'," he continued. "They ain't got much and I figured she'd fancy a new dress."

Winright took another sip of the whiskey and proffered the jug to Elisha, who made no move to accept it.

"You'd better stay away from up there," Elisha warned. "Clary's boys might not take it any better than Belle did."

"Hell, Lige, you know the way I am," Winright countered. "Ain't nobody goin' to keep me away from what's mine."

"That's just it, son; she ain't yours. Her daddy's in his grave."

"But Lige . . ."

"No buts about it, man," Elisha interrupted. "Leave the past alone. That family don't need no more grief."

"Now Lige, you know I ain't goin' to let no woman tell me what to do," Winright said defiantly.

Elisha continued his withering stare at his visitor and walked over to him, placing the corncob back into the whiskey jug Winright held.

"Listen to me," he said, quietly but firmly. "You'd best take that jug and go on home. No charge. And I'm goin' to give you some free advice too. Don't trifle with Belle. You go back up to Clary's and she will kill you."

Winright recoiled as if he had been mildly slapped, but took the reins of his horse to turn it around on the narrow path. He put a foot into the stirrup and swung his long legs over the saddle, cradling the whiskey like a baby in his arms.

"I don't know if I can do that, Lige," he said more softly now. "I do have some responsibility here."

Elisha eyes did not blink when he spoke again: "Winright, you're Phoebe's nephew. You're family, and I'm tellin' you this as an uncle and a friend. Don't go back to Clary's. If you want to give something to Adelaide, you give it to all the children. You bring it to me and I'll take it to them."

"Now, Lige," Winright said dismissively, although there was a hint of nervousness in his voice. "You think Belle actually would try to kill me for somethin' like that?"

"No, she wouldn't try, God damn it," Elisha said. "She'd kill you graveyard dead."

"Ahh, I . . . I'll study on it," Winright said, looking away from Elisha's glare.

Elisha took the reins of Winright's horse as he drew a final, steely bead on the younger man's eyes, locking onto them. Winright knew he was about to say something important and did not move, awaiting Elisha's pronouncement.

"Listen to me, son" he began. "Don't go back up there again."

Elisha spoke carefully and slowly, making sure that Winright heard every word: "I can't change the past and you can't either. I got to live with it. You got to live with it, too. You understand me?"

Winright said nothing, but nodded affirmatively.

"Now you understand this," Elisha continued. "You bother that little girl again, and if Belle don't kill you, I swear I will."

Winright was momentarily taken aback; Elisha was certainly not a young man anymore, but he was still formidable. There was power in what he said. He could see the fire in Elisha's coal-black eyes and for a harrowing moment it seemed that it was not Elisha standing in front of him, but Zachariah in all his fury, just before he shot him dead. But somehow he knew that if he fired again, it would not stop him this time, that it would not be Zachariah bleeding to death on his cabin floor. He had long ago learned that Elisha Hopkins did not make idle threats; he was nothing if not a man of his word and when he released the horse's reins, he stepped back a pace and stood up straight, awaiting Winright's reaction.

In another time, Winright Adkins would have leapt from the saddle and confronted any man who dared challenge him. He would have fought such a man with gun or knife or bare fists, but he knew that this was Elisha Hopkins who was speaking to him, and if he did shoot him, the Indians would cut his throat before he made it to the bottom of the hill. But more importantly, he realized the time for recklessness was past, at least for him, and he no longer wanted to be part of the fury he could sense in so many eyes, the fury still raging just under the surface all over Greasy Creek, all over Pike County.

Ain't nobody needs any more of that, he thought.

After a pause, he nodded again, in subtle compliance, and gently touched his horse's flanks to begin the journey back down off Ripley Knob.

When he got to a bend in the path, he stopped to look back, just before Elisha and his still went out of sight.

That old man will never die, Winright thought. He is as tough as those big old trees.

He knew Elisha Hopkins would never have said what he did unless he meant it. And he accepted the wisdom of the advice he was given. Except in passing, he would never see Adelaide Phillips again and he would never more speak of her as long as he lived.

Chapter Eight

Redbud Winter

Every year the redbuds are the first to bloom on Greasy Creek; they announce themselves with only the briefest prompting, when the sun itself is yet too timid to confront the dying season. Wise gardeners have already put out their peas on Groundhog Day, as the tradition holds, and do not fear the last of winter's rages. But they will reserve their tender plants until dogwood and blackberry winters are past, because they are wise. They know the dangers of impatience, of investing in the soil too soon, and mark the redbuds' arrival only as the signal to buy seeds or sketch out garden plots, and they wait in warm kitchens for the last of the late snows and frosts to burn away. They know spring is faithless in the mountains, even though its warm days are like rude trollops trying to lure them outside with promises of greater sunshine. But the wise will wait, because they know spring will slip away in the night, leaving half-finished roofs covered with snow or garden hoses frozen like petrified snakes.

In the mountains, we are taught such caution by our elders, who were taught by their elders, wisdom passed down through generations to ensure that the race survived, and we do not expect to see hoary heads making extravagant plans when spring will not offer any guarantees. We would never expect old people to be out in the fields before it was time or suddenly decide to move to a new home while half the creek was still covered with ice. So it troubled Mammy in the spring of 1904, when she heard that Elisha had sent his boys up to Ripley Knob to clean out the cabin that had not been occupied in years.

What's that old fool up to now, she wondered? It's just redbud winter.

She had heard the word from George W. Blackburn's wife, after she had inquired about Lila, who had just had Harrison's latest child. Like her father, she was born with a cleft palate and her right foot was twisted and misshapen. The shock was palpable for everyone in the house, but Mammy forbade any weeping. There was something about the child's eyes that struck Mammy immediately. This is the one, she thought. This is the one I been waiting for. They named her Rissie and she cooed to Mammy as her grandmother washed away the excess of her birth.

"Welcome to your new home, little girl," Mammy said. "You got a good life ahead of you. Old Mammy will see to that."

"They can fix her mouth now," she told her heartbroken son. "I'll have it fixed myself. This baby will have a good life."

Harrison believed her, even though life had not been easy for the Hopkinses in the last years, and for a time Mammy herself had forgotten when it had ever been. The family was breaking up; the older ones dying and the younger ones moving away. Like so many of Greasy Creek's people, the old ways were disappearing, too.

In 1880, Matilda Hopkins Robinson died and was buried next to Samuel in the old Hopkins cemetery where the first of the family dead were laid. She was the last to be placed there, because she reserved her place beside the man she loved. The family no longer owned the land, but the new Prater owners gladly permitted the Hopkinses to bury their dead there or on the new cemetery higher up on the hill, behind the cabin where Cornelius and Dorcus lived out their final days. The family did not plan to bury anyone else in the old burying ground, but made an exception the following year.

In 1881, John Miles Hopkins, the only son of Confederate soldier Joseph Hopkins, died of fever. A doctor in Pikeville might have saved him, but the family had no money to pay for a doctor's visit, and John Miles was too sick to travel. It was also doubtful he would have lived until he got there; the disease had ravaged Greasy Creek and the hammering of boards and tacking of cloth onto them could be heard nightly as other families prepared to bury their dead. John Miles sickened the same day his youngest daughter died and passed away as visitors were paying their respects to the infant in the homemade coffin in the other room. His wife buried them in the same grave beside Victoria, since all that was left of the Shelby Creek farm was Lucinda's widow's dowry, and none of their family would lie in the soil that once gave them unimaginable wealth.

Mammy would have objected to his burial in the new cemetery anyway; the owner of the land had faced Joseph at Saltville and she would not countenance his son's remains to be placed near where Ezekiel Prater would eventually be buried. It bothered Zeke Prater that she felt that way, but he knew the animosities of the War died hard on Greasy Creek.

The old soldiers themselves had mellowed with age. Two years after John Miles's death, Winright Adkins decided that Cornelius's old cabin would no longer do for a church building and gave the Greasy Creek Old Regular Baptist Church a spot of land on down Greasy Creek, the same property where the church still sits. The cabin on the Old Prater Cemetery, as it was now called, was falling down, and Winright helped the church members dismantle it. However, they also built a stand the church still used in summertime for a hundred years, until the new road took away all traces of the stand or the cemetery itself in 2003.

The new church building recently had work done on its heating system, but if the members were to review their deed, they would find that Winright also gave them the eternal right to gather firewood from his hillside. Although it is doubtful that the church will ever return to stoves to warm its members, it illustrates how much Winright had changed after he spoke to Elisha about Adelaide. He died later in the same year as Elisha, and was said to have asked for a final forgiveness on his deathbed. Since the War, death was omnipresent, and the people of Greasy Creek, like other Pike Countians, had been overwhelmed with the sheer number of people who died, during the War or afterward from wounds or illness from the War, or simply from broken hearts, and the sanctuary of the church was sorely needed.

There had also been a boom in marriages and births since the War ended, and the church members saw a gradual supplanting of the sad reasons for its formation. A younger generation was growing up without direct memories of the madness and cruelty that had ravaged the mountains not even a generation before. Robert Damron eventually felt he could wean himself away from the Greasy Creek institution, and new preachers began to fill the pews behind the rostrum.

With the freedom to walk Greasy Creek's roads without harassment, Adelaide joined Mammy on a great quest to plant flowers on soldiers' graves up and down the creek, beginning with Zachariah's. She also became her father's greatest partisan, regardless of the fact he had not truly sired her, and she dismissed forever any thoughts to the contrary. She would never miss an opportunity to proudly speak of his Confederate service, reminding everyone that "my daddy was with President Davis at the end."

The stories about the early Decoration Days on Greasy Creek were legion. One venerable matron told me that when she was a child, my great-grandfather, Harrison Hopkins, came walking by her house one warm spring day, carrying garden tools, when her mother invited him in for some cold tea. As he sat on the porch with Clarinda Williams, daughter of Adelaide Phillips Sanders, he looked down at the young girl sitting at his feet and asked her if she had seen her Granny Adelaide that day.

"She's gone to the cemetery with Mammy," she replied. "It's Decoration Day don't you know?"

But of course he did; Mammy and Adelaide would not let anyone forget. The two women had become a formidable team, almost sisters, even though Mammy had helped Clarinda Phillips birth the younger woman. Adelaide knew the stories of the two moonstruck cousins, Belle and Victoria, and the men they loved, and knew she could never replace Victoria in Mammy's eyes, but together they decorated the graves of the Phillips children and Victoria, and she would turn her head when Mammy began to weep.

Harrison smiled, and his great mustache barely moved as he spoke: "Seetheart, let me thell you something: your grandm-mother and my m-mother are covering m-me up with flowers."

Harrison had just come from the cemeteries, after working for the past three days clearing away the brush and weeds mounding up the graves. It was an annual tradition now; Mammy had marshaled the men of the creek into action years before, demanding they pick up their scythes and hoes to clean the cemeteries and build fences around them. While some of the men reluctantly turned to their duties, others gladly signed onto the work parties.

The young, unmarried men were especially helpful after they learned that Mammy's outings to the graveyards gave them a socially acceptable opportunity to meet eligible young women as they placed the flowers they had so lovingly prepared. And at the dinners Mammy would prepare for the workers after they had finished their annual toil, there would be another opportunity for conversation. Mammy's house soon became the main location on Greasy Creek for the younger set to meet and often marry the man or woman of their dreams. A look at the marriage licenses issued to Greasy Creek residents after the War reveal an inordinate number of marriages held at the home of Dorcus Hopkins.

Or Dorcus Hopkins Lewis, for Mammy herself finally married.

In 1879, at about the same time Elisha married for the last time, another wedding took place at Mammy's place. Twenty-three year old Henry Lewis of Floyd County married thirty-year-old Mary Marshall, formerly of Russell County, Virginia in Mammy's living room. Henry was fairly wealthy for an Eastern Kentuckian at the time, having received an inheritance from his Philadelphia grandfather, a rich merchant who staked Henry's father to a mercantile business on the Ohio River at Catlettsburg, and set up Henry with his own business up the river in Prestonsburg. Henry met Mary on one of his frequent steamboat trips delivering goods up the Big Sandy and fell in love immediately. Mammy noticed that the difference in the lovers' ages made no difference to Henry.

In 1881, Mary died in childbirth, and Henry turned to Mammy to help him raise his son. It was neither an unfamiliar nor an unwelcome task for her. Before long, Henry moved in with Mammy and she became a Lewis, supposedly after a marriage and honeymoon in Cincinnati. Not everyone was sure she was actually married, but no one would deny her a final chance at happiness. The couple had no children of their own, but were content with raising their sons, her two and his one, all of which were cooed over by the young girls that made Mammy's place their second home. At Mammy's place, the feuds, the violence, and the poverty of post-Civil War Pike County would be forgotten. Long after Mammy died, Rissie kept the tradition alive at her own home.

A cousin of mine once told me that all the kids of Greasy Creek went to Rissie's because "she was liberal" for those days. "We used to go up there to have popcorn and listen to the radio," she said. "But we actually just wanted to meet boys." I suspect Mammy's ghost was there with them, smiling at the legacy she had left them.

But if Mammy could offer the young people of Greasy Creek sanctuary from the hateful world around them as the new century approached, she could not offer the same respite to her father, who was fading as the century waned. As a new generation of boys and girls grew up, they largely forgot the old man on Ripley Knob.

Columbus Christopher Hopkins, his younger brother, joined the Grand Army of the Republic when the lodge was formed in Pikeville. Columbus no longer saw a reason to deny his part in the effort that saved the Union, even if it took his brother's life. Elisha, who had tried so hard to keep his family out of the War, did not oppose his brother's move, but it was disconcerting to him that marches were organized and bands played in Pikeville and the entire country would honor what he had fought so hard against, would honor what had taken so many lives.

It must have puzzled him that the War mattered little to the new generation that had been born since the War and that had no direct memories of it, only what their elders had told them. They had other concerns as they tried to make a living on plots of land that grew progressively smaller each time a father's homestead was divided with his death. Some men saw hope for their families dwindling on Greasy Creek and began to look to other places to live, far from Pike County and even far from Kentucky. Pike County's narrow valleys had only a finite amount of bottomland, and it was needed for crops for the living. As the old soldiers died, they were taken farther up on the ridges for burial. But they were not forgotten, due to Mammy's efforts and the recognition throughout the country that all of them deserved to be honored.

Southern states had already passed laws creating Decoration Days to remember their fallen soldiers, and the GAR had established its own day of remembrance in 1868, placing flowers on all Union and Confederate soldiers buried at Arlington. The practice rapidly spread. In 1873, New York's legislature passed laws establishing such a day and by 1890, all the Northern states had followed suit. As the nineteenth century came to a close in Pike County, the animosities of the Civil War no longer seemed sufficient grounds to take a man's life, or more, perhaps the old soldiers simply found themselves too feeble to draw a weapon anymore. Occasionally, gray-bearded men who had once tried to kill each other in their manhood could be seen standing with their arms locked to each other as old comrades or old enemies were lowered into the earth. In their advanced age they were chums again, as they were in childhood, before the War tore them apart.

But Elisha could never forget and became more embittered and isolated, and he resisted every effort to bring him back into the Greasy Creek society that was re-establishing itself.

At first he was content to live on his mountain with his new family, although Mammy plagued him with demands that he send the boys to school. After the birth of her last child in 1889, the same year that Lila married Harrison, Mary decided she had played the role of mother for too long and wanted some relief from the monotony of life on Ripley Knob. Elisha was seventy-four when his last child was born, and could no longer keep up with the sexual demands of his wife. Eventually, she turned to others to satisfy her needs, and Elisha seemed no longer to care. On the odd occasion that one of his grandchildren or great-grandchildren came to visit, he would usually ignore them and return to his still. Before long, the infrequent visits stopped completely. The only visitors Elisha welcomed were his Indian friends, and one day they disappeared as well.

By 1890, Elisha, who once owned vast tracts of Greasy Creek through his accumulation of land grants, had sold off nearly everything he had, except for Ripley Knob. While he kept the land, he sold the trees. Timber speculators had been coming into the hills for years, looking for trees to feed the building boom that was rolling across America, and the Yellow Poplar Lumber Company of Ironton, Ohio bought up nearly all the timber on Greasy Creek. They built a narrow-gauge railroad to haul away the timber and hired local boys and their mules to cut down the trees and haul them off the mountains. The tiny railway cut into the hillside above the falls where Greasy Creek's children swam and pushed dirt into the pool, almost covering the great flat rock they dived off. It was the first of many concessions the people of Greasy Creek would make.

For a while, the money was good, but the landowners did not realize what they had signed until the timber company finished cutting their land, leaving only ugly, barren hillsides covered with rotting stumps. Some of the landowners attempted to take the timber company to court, but the courts found that the deeds gave the company sweeping rights to the trees, including the right to remove any and all trees in any way they chose. "You should have read your deed before you signed it," the judges universally said, to men who could not read or write their own names and signed documents with a mark. But the judges and the Kentucky legislature, their purses fattened by money from the timber and coal speculators, always took the side of industry, claiming a greater good would be achieved by denying mountaineers their rights.

The Indians were aghast at what they saw: every day more of the great trees fell. The Cherokee had lived in Pike County for generations, some coming before the federal government forced them off their native lands in Georgia and North Carolina in 1838, and some coming afterward, escaping the horror of the Trail of Tears. They had lived quietly, and rarely had a deed to the land on which they lived, the land on which they died, and where they buried their dead, and they were powerless to stop the destruction. It was more than mere trees that were cut down and hauled away to them; it was the repository of their gods, of the spirits of their people, and they could do nothing more than stare at the holocaust swirling around them. Every day, they would stand near the cutting and watch the great trees fall; they would watch the hapless mules strain to haul their burden down to the tracks where the train awaited them, like undertakers receiving a corpse, and they watched the trees leave the place where they had grown untouched for hundreds of years.

Every night, they would return to their homes and grieve like they would have grieved for loved ones, like they grieved for the boys who had gone away to war and never returned. They grieved like they were grieving for the loss of their very souls. By 1900, the People could no longer claim Greasy Creek as their home, and without a word to anyone except Elisha, they disappeared.

The Indians were not the only ones to go away. Around 1890, Zachariah's oldest son John lost his first wife to another round of fever. There were still few doctors in Pike County and little money to pay them, and as Greasy Creek became crowded, disease began to take its toll. John married again, but came to his Clarinda's house one day to tell his mother that he was leaving. He was going to Oregon, to begin a whole new life before he grew too old. He said there was a better chance of making a living there, he told her, at least a living without fear there, and he kissed her goodbye for the last time.

"I ain't got no choice, Mother," he said. "It won't ever get no better here."

Clarinda knew what he said was true, and feared for the day she would be told that John had killed Winright for the killing of his father. She knew that ancient debt was part of why John was leaving. Now she had only Joe to worry about until she died.

"Will you write to me?" she asked.

"Yes, ma'am," he said. "You know I will."

But he came back only once, to see her grave. She died the same year as Elisha and Winright, and was buried in the place she had reserved beside her husband forty years earlier.

Clarinda was not the first mother on Greasy Creek to say good-bye in such a way; mothers have been saying such good-byes to their children for more than a hundred years in these hills. Families had moved away from Greasy Creek since the end of the War and the out-migration still occurs, as regularly as the high schools in Pike County disgorge their young, although a few still return to visit or to die in the bosom of the hills where they were born. They prefer to come in spring, and spring in Pike County is still a time when the hillsides burst with the promise of new growth and new hope, but real hope is still largely found elsewhere, even though the trees have finally come back. Not the great trees that once grew here for a thousand years, but at least the hillsides are covered again, until the strip mines push them down, along with the mountains that are their foundation.

Without the trees and without the blooms from the great poplars, the honey Elisha used for his signature whiskey was no more, and neither was the whiskey itself, but he no longer cared about that either. In the year before the old century died, he appeared at the house of George W. Blackburn and asked him for thirty dollars to pay his debts and a house to live in until he died. If his son would take care of him, he would give him the deed for the last property he had on Greasy Creek, the cabin on Ripley Knob.

George W. looked at his father and his new family in pity; the lawsuit I discovered, a lawsuit that Elisha's last children filed in an unsuccessful attempt to regain Ripley Knob, said their clothing was ragged and it was obvious that they were starving. George W. agreed to his father's terms if Mary would give up her profligate life. The lawsuit said she was "notoriously unchaste." That was probably why the family never spoke of her. Venereal disease was rampant at the turn of the century in Pike County, and the accepted treatment for syphilis, arsenic therapy, killed as many as it cured. She died three years after Elisha did, still a relatively young woman. Reading between the lines of the suit, it is easy to infer that she was too ill to take care of herself, let alone Elisha and her three sons.

It is ironic that Elisha, whose character was in such opposition to the biblical prophet his mother named him for, would have found a Jezebel at last, but I do not believe he would have considered her such. Nor would he have considered himself virtuous; I suspect he would have forgiven her because of his own deeds, although she may simply have not mattered to him anymore. But when their son Will died in 1959, he was taken, according to his wishes, back to Ripley Knob to be buried beside his mother and father.

When Will was in the final stages of Parkinson's disease and could no longer hold a spoon to feed himself, he moved in with Rissie and ignored the pleas of his own children to go with them to their home in Indiana. He said he had been born on Greasy Creek and that's where he would die.

"They're goin' to lay me next to Mommy and Daddy," he said, as if he were a child and not an old man. There had to have been some love between his parents for him to remember them so fondly.

Will never spoke of Mary's fondness for men, and not all the last years of Elisha Hopkins were unhappy. Although he evidenced no pride in their union, Elisha did not attempt to prevent it when Harrison and Lila fell in love and were married. Elisha attended the wedding, but resumed his denigration of his hare-lipped grandson afterward. Mammy ignored Elisha and tried to make Harrison do the same.

"He's just a crazy old man," she told him. "You pay no attention to him, and Mammy'll straighten him out."

She did eventually, before he died, and in his own way, Elisha asked Harrison to forgive him. Mammy wanted that for her father's sake, in case he needed some help on Judgment Day, but her thoughts were now focused on her children.

When her grandchildren by Harrison and Lila arrived, Mammy was beside herself with happiness.

At last my sweet boy will find some happiness, she thought.

In 1893, Joseph, her second son, married and again she was overjoyed.

I'll have me some more grandchildren, she thought. He'll tell them the stories I told him and the family'll tell them forever.

But before the children came, Joseph died too.

He had taken his first corn crop to Powell's Mills, not far above Greasy Creek, and went swimming as the grain was being ground into cornmeal. The pool was wide and deep behind the dam that filled the narrow opening to Powell's Creek, and it was a popular spot for the boys of Pike County to swim. Joseph swam there often, and was considered one of the best swimmers on Greasy Creek or maybe even all of Pike County. He was strong and healthy and had perfect lips that smiled often.

He'll tell the stories, she thought. He'll keep the stories alive.

But when the grinding was over and the barrels were filled, the proprietors of the mill went looking for Joseph and found him floating in the millpond.

I know nothing of her grief; no spirits whispered to me the magnitude of her loss, and Mammy, as stoic as she had to be, would not have revealed it to me. But she had depended on young Joe to tell the stories of the family, and she must have mourned for that loss almost as much as she mourned her son's passing. I learned that after he died, she gave away all her colorful bonnets and wore only black for the rest of her life. For nearly a decade, she grieved that there would be no one to tell the stories of Elisha, of Joseph, of Zachariah, of the Old Ones.

But fate did not leave Mammy without hope. After she demanded that Elisha square himself with Harrison, Rissie came along. Although she was stricken with the same harelip as her father, there was something different about this child. She could see it in the bright eyes that twinkled above the ruined mouth. She took Rissie's cleft palate as a sign, and Mammy knew that even with it, Rissie would be the one to tell the stories and she could go to her own grave, certain that they would never be lost.

Almost on the day Rissie was born, Elisha Hopkins announced he was moving back to Ripley Knob. Some people thought the old man was mad, but no one could dissuade him; it was as if he had summoned once more the unbounded energy of his youth, and he even spoke of plans to put in a crop.

There is sometimes a strange phenomenon in terminal illnesses; people who the day before had struggled to take a breath will leave their sickbeds and walk around the room as if nothing was wrong. They will eat a meal or take a drink or laugh again, but it lasts only briefly as the body sends its last reserves of adrenaline out to fight off the inevitable. Perhaps that was what happened to Elisha in the early spring of 1904 as he sent his sons back to Ripley Knob to clean out the cabin for his return. Perhaps he had that last burst of vigor and did not know he was near death. He was almost ninety years old, yet seriously believed he could start life all over again. He thanked George W. for his help and marched upright down Main Greasy Creek to the base of the mountain where, on the brow above, he had built a cabin with his brother, where he had taken his first wife for their honeymoon, and where he had also taken his last wife nearly half a century later. As he walked up the mountain like a young man, the redbuds were blooming, as they do every year in the mountains, heralding the promise of spring with a fine, royal coat of purple, gently covering with a fleeting grace the last scars of winter.

For the last time in his life, Elisha was home, where he had always been happiest, and where long ago he determined he would die. That's what he's goin' back for, Mammy thought, and made no effort to stop him.

Three months later, she walked into her yard and drew out her pipe and tobacco, climbed the steps to her front porch and sat down in her rocker to smoke as the rest of her father's funeral party traipsed down from Ripley Knob. She had stayed with them until the first clumps of earth had been spilled onto the old man's coffin, but then climbed onto her horse for the journey to the valley floor. She knew Elisha's sons would complete the work on the mountaintop and she had her own work to do.

Mammy had been cooking since the night before and had been up since long before daylight, preparing small mountains of food for the guests, as the custom on Greasy Creek had always been, and on this day she wanted to make sure everything was done well.

"Mammy, do you want me to put out the butter?" one of the girls scurrying about the yard asked her.

"No, baby," she replied. "Leave it in the springhouse for now. Wait till they all get here."

The girl quickly turned back to her duties.

She's a good baby, Mammy thought; they were all good babies. I guess I didn't do too bad in all these years. This one's one of Haley's granddaughters, which she never got to see, God bless her. She never knew her Mamaw and probably don't know much about her Papaw either, and she probably don't want to know much more. I guess it's too late to tell her now. But I'll tell this one, she thought, looking at Rissie, her infant granddaughter sleeping peacefully in the cradle beside her, her separated upper lip bubbling as she breathed. I'll have that fixed, Baby Girl, she thought. There weren't no money to have your daddy's fixed, but I'll fix yours, and I'll tell you about your family and you'll keep the memories always.

Before she went to Ripley Knob for the funeral that morning, Mammy set up tables under the trees that ringed her lawn, and now they were filled with bowls and baskets of food, all covered with clean sheets to keep flies away.

The girls did good, she thought, I may have taught them something after all.

She was pleased with her handiwork. The mourners would remember this feast, and Elisha deserved at least that much.

As they filed down from the mountain, some on foot and some on horses, she took note of the crowd that was gathering across the creek from her home. More people had come than she expected, and she hoped the number indicated respect instead of mere curiosity, but she was ready for them. They began to drift toward the whitewashed picket fence that surrounded her house, and the girls who had been working so diligently preparing the tables made a last survey of their offerings and moved toward Mammy's porch, awaiting her orders. Likewise the crowd hesitated before opening the gate, although the women who, as was the custom, would eat last, came directly into the yard and joined the girls at Mammy's feet. The men remained outside, keeping a respectful distance and waiting for the cue to be received.

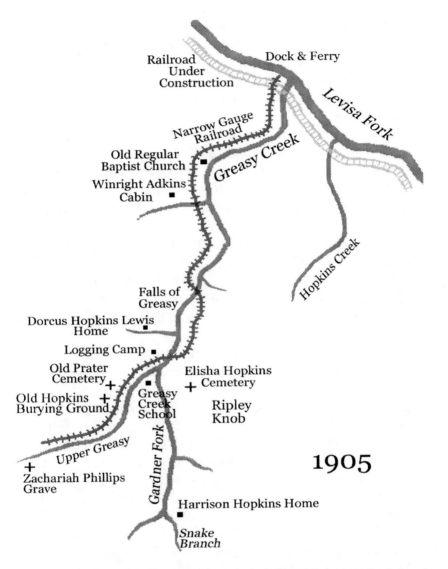

By 1905 a school and a church occupy the site of Elisha's farm at the forks of Greasy Creek, and a narrow-gauge railroad extends the length of Greasy Creek. Built by the Yellow Poplar Lumber Company of Ironton, Ohio, the narrow-gauge carried to the river the great yellow poplar logs that once dominated the creek (and whose blooms gave rise to the honey Elisha used for his brew). A new coal railroad is under construction. The Greasy Creek Old Regular Baptist Church has been enjoying its new home for nearly twenty years, but in summer, services are still held on the Old Prater Cemetery.

"Go get the butter and buttermilk now," she whispered to the girls nearest her. "The rest of you take the covers off the tables," she ordered the others. At once the girls and women responded and the men, seeing the commotion in Dorcus's yard, began filing through the gate. All of them came by her porch to remove or tip their hats in acknowledgement.

From her vantage point, she could see the last of the men come down from the mountain and, except for George, all of them made a beeline for her yard. George, riding the mare Dorcus had lent him, turned up the creek instead. There was another gravesite he had to visit and his daughter, now a grown woman with her own children, rode beside him with her husband. They lived on Johns Creek, not far from where Elisha and Haley had lived for a while, and would be riding out of Greasy Creek when her father did.

Mammy knew they would not concern themselves with dinner this day, and she had already packed them baskets to take home.

Forty years, she thought, and that part of his soul was still quick, and it will be until the day he dies.

She saw that George had brought some of Elisha's flowers off the hill with him; flowers that would adorn a much older grave, albeit of a much younger person.

The stacks of fried chicken on the tables quickly tumbled under the onslaught of the men, and the bowls of dumplings were rapidly and repeatedly emptied. Pones of cornbread disappeared as soon as they were broken and the girls made frequent trips to the garden for more tomatoes and cucumbers, which also vanished as soon as they were put to the knife. They'll remember this meal if nothing else, Mammy thought.

As the men finished eating, they drifted to various parts of her yard and produced an occasional bottle to share or knives from their pockets to trade among themselves. A few came by to offer a final word to Mammy before they left, but most of them waited for George to return. By the time the last of the women sat down to eat, George and Rebecca Victoria, along with her husband, appeared riding slowly up to Mammy's gate.

Sixty-four years old he is, she thought, still a handsome man, and still a sad one. And Becky . . . so beautiful. She's . . . what . . . thirty-nine now? Older than her mother lived to be. Victoria would be so proud of her, of both of them.

The deep bass voice of the steamboat down on the river at the mouth of Greasy Creek rumbled its way up the valley, as if announcing their entry as they entered the compound. After shaking hands with family and friends who awaited them, George and his daughter walked over to Mammy's porch and went up the steps to embrace her as she sat smoking her pipe.

"That's the boat, Sister," he said. "I got to be goin' now."

Mammy rose from her chair and picked up the basket of food she had saved for him and put her arms around him as he took it.

"You take this with you, Brother," she said, with a kiss on his cheek. "You might get hungry goin' home."

Then she turned to Rebecca Victoria.

"Becky," she said. "Come here and give your old Mammy a hug before you go."

Becky dutifully kissed her aunt on her cheek and then tightly embraced her. Mammy held her close for a moment.

"You still got your Mommy's eyes," she said, smiling. "You ever want to know what she looked like, you look in the mirror. But I told you that before, hain't I?"

"Yes, ma'am," she replied. "You have many times."

Harrison came around the house with Mammy's horse and waited for George to take leave of the assembly. He would ride with him to the river and return with the horse after he boarded. George took his daughter's hand and walked down the steps toward Harrison. He gave her a final embrace before he shook hands with his son-in-law and took the horse's reins from Harrison.

"When you comin' back, Brother?" Mammy asked him.

"I'll be back by fall," he replied. "Before long, I'll be able to ride a train up here anytime I want. They say the railroad will be in Pikeville next year. I can ride it out of Prestonsburg right now."

He looked around at Mammy's yard and the friends and family that had come to say good-bye to his father. "It's a good crowd, Sister," he said. "Reckon Pappy would be proud they come?"

"He wouldn't give a damn either way," Mammy smiled. "You know that. But I'm glad they all come."

He gave the reins back to Harrison and came back up the steps to clasp her in his arms one final time. Although he said nothing, she could feel his chest heave as he suppressed a sob and then he went down the steps and mounted the horse to ride away. George smiled at her and lifted his hat one last time before he and Harrison disappeared around the bend of the creek.

With George's exit, the guests began to disperse and the girls began cleaning up the tables behind them and washing dishes and feeding the hogs with table scraps. Before long, almost everyone had departed and there was little left to remind anyone that a dinner had been held here, or that a legend had been buried that day. By the time Harrison returned with the horse, Lila had already collected Rissie and the rest of her children, along with her mother, and returned to her home. Mammy spoke to Harrison as he led the horses to the barn.

"Harrison," she said. "If it don't rain tomorrow, you and some of the men take the wagons up to Lige's cabin and get everything out of it. Then you nail it shut."

"Yes, ma'am," he said. "I told Will we'd go back up and get what was left." Harrison spoke precisely and the great mustache that hid his cleft palate barely moved.

Will and his two brothers were waiting for Harrison by the gate, and they followed him to his house, where their sickly mother awaited them. None of them expected it to be long before she joined her husband.

Those boys love him, she thought, they call him "Uncle," though by rights he's their nephew, or half-nephew. Damn you, Lige, with all your women, nobody'll ever figure all this out, but it don't matter no more.

Mary would never return to the cabin she shared with Elisha until she died, Mammy knew, and then Elisha would have all his wives with him for eternity. Except for one, of course, the one he loved the most, the one who was first reclaimed by the earth.

Henry pushed open the screen door and came out on the porch, carrying his tobacco pouch. He sat down beside her and filled his pipe, tamping down the aromatic mixture and lighting it. They sat without speaking and smoked as the last light departed the nearly barren valley and the whippoorwills began their evening serenade.

"At least we still got a few quail around," he said, making conversation.

"A few," she replied.

"You did good today, old girl," he complimented her. In the twilight, he could see her nod in acknowledgement. After a pause, he spoke again: "Well, are you comin' to bed?"

"You know, Henry, I sometimes wish you could have come here before the War," Mammy said wistfully, not responding to his question. "Greasy Creek was a right pretty place then; we had all those trees. We were happy."

"Ain't you happy now?" he asked her lightly. "You're married to me. Don't I make you happy?"

"Then the War came . . ." she continued.

"Well, look what's comin' now," he said. "Railroad comin' in, mines openin'. There'll be plenty of work for all these boys. They won't have to go away now."

"Henry," she said, breaking the trance she was falling into. "I want some of your money to get Rissie's mouth fixed before she gets older. If the doctors can't fix her here, I'll take her to Cincinnati if I have to."

"Whatever you want, Belle," he laughed. "I don't reckon you spent all of it yet."

"She's got to tell the stories," Mammy continued. "Ain't nobody else goin' to. She has to have a good mouth."

"Anything you want," he said, smilling. "Are you ready to go to bed now?"

"I want it done," she said firmly.

The fireflies had come out, as if luring the moon with their twinkling, and Mammy looked up a final time at Ripley Knob, where her father lay, where the trees once grew, and where a nearly forgotten way of life was now entombed. It appeared to Henry that she was searching for something on that mountain, but did not know what she was looking for.

Finally, she seemed to accept that there was nothing to be revealed to her and sighed. There would be no sweet music from an angel band on that mountain for her to hear, no luminescence from ancient ghosts to welcome the man who had walked so tall among them. But she knew that she would not have been privy to such things anyway, not as long as she was still among the living.

But there would be others near his grave this night, she knew. Joe and Zack would be there, and Haley. And so many others; they would come for him, she knew, even if she could not discern their presences, for the living are not always allowed to see these things.

"All right, old man," she finally said. "Let's go to bed."

She looked at her husband as they rose together, tapping their pipes on the porch rail and emptying the ashes into the darkness. The door spring screeched briefly in protest as he opened the door for her and he followed her in.

Sometime during the night, she rose again and looked once more at the mountain, ghostly and pale in the moonlight, when the clouds parted to let her see it, for the rain was approaching. If she saw anything there, she told no one, and before morning, the rain began. Two days later, when the trail had dried, Harrison hitched his team to the wagon and, with Elisha's last three sons, made his way to the ancient cabin and its newly mounded grave.

When they got there, they were astounded to find a rude shelter of branches and bark erected over the bare earth and an odd feathered device hanging above it from the branch of a nearby tree. Tiny feathers, white and yellow, alternating with somewhat larger, bright blue ones lined a grapevine ring, and attached at the bottom were larger, full white feathers with a single, huge, dark brown specimen hanging down and gently turning in the wind. So dark it was nearly black for most of its length, it had a brilliant white tip. No one on that hill had seen such a feather before, and no one had the first idea of where it came from.

"What is this, Uncle Harrison?" Will asked as he took it down from the tree. "Is this an eagle feather?"

Harrison studied the device intently and looked back at the grave shelter. He shook his head, puzzled at what he saw.

"Should we take this down to Mammy?" Will asked. "Would she know what it is?"

"No," Harrison said, gently placing the artifact back on the tree. "Whoever p-put it here did it for a reason. I think we'd b-best leave it." It hung there motionless as they worked until the wagon was loaded and the cabin door nailed shut.

A soft breeze was rising when they mounted the wagon and started down the mountain road to the valley floor. Harrison raised himself off the seat to keep pressure on the brake when the path sharply dipped. When it leveled again and just before the cabin went out of sight, he stopped for a final look.

If that old place could talk, he thought, the stories it could tell.

He released the brake and clucked to the team, which began obediently plodding forward with its cargo. Harrison and the boys turned their eyes to the road as Ripley Knob finally slipped out of sight.

Although they could not see it, in the faint wind a nearly imperceptible movement of the ring had begun. In a moment it began to sway back and forth, rhythmically and purposefully, as if it was part of some ancient ritual, as if the hand of some spectral priest had taken it up like a holy censer. And in the company of angels and spirits and all the souls of Greasy Creek, whatever hand that moved it accepted and consecrated the fresh grave below.

Epilogue: The Indian

*A*lmost a quarter-century ago, some eighty years after the last Indians left Greasy Creek, workmen in the city of Pikeville were digging a new gas line to a church on Main Street. They found a series of flat, overlapping rocks, and after moving away one of the stones, uncovered what appeared to be a rotted mat. One of them jumped nearly out of the hole when he pulled it back and saw what lay beneath. It was a perfectly preserved skull, which immediately dropped its jaw down on its bony chest, as if in awe of the daylight it had not seen in centuries.

The coroner was called and the rest of the skeleton was uncovered. I was called as well. I was between teaching jobs, working in television news, and skeletal remains were always a good story. I can still recall my amazement at the stunned look of that skull, if a skeleton can offer expression.

With every bone present, it was so well preserved that the coroner first thought it was the lost grave of a white man, maybe even an unreported murder, although the bits of pottery and arrowheads that shared the grave indicated it was an Indian. The skeleton was carefully removed and sent to the state medical examiner's office in Louisville. A few weeks later, the ME released his report, which said that it was indeed Indian, but not Cherokee, and had been buried long before they came into the hills. It was from another time and of another race of the People and was possibly six to eight hundred years old.

I did a follow-up story on the report, and went on with my work, thinking in passing that one of these days I ought to explore the history of this region. I had never seen Indians, except in movies, and was surprised to learn they once lived here.

The report also noted that the skeleton had been given to a "Native American" organization for reburial. It was the first use I had seen of a politically correct term. No one knows where it was taken, and that may have been deliberate, although some rumors circulated that Indians were seen in Pikeville and were planning a ceremony in honor of the warrior we found. There was also talk that the Indians were angry because we had taken pictures, and that a curse had been placed on the town, but no one believed it and nothing especially tragic happened, at least nothing more than the town was accustomed to. After a few lunchtime conversations, interest faded and the town returned to its business, although some citizens kept a wary eye out for dark-haired transients, and one of the workmen who kept a piece of the Indian's pottery swore that it remained strangely warm to the touch.

Today that story is largely forgotten, for the mountain town is growing at a pace like no other time in its history, and looking mostly to the future, with grand new buildings going up almost daily. In its expansion, more such graves may be found. The town has long outgrown the old boundary of the river, which defined it for a hundred years, until bridges replaced ferries as the twentieth century began. Almost into its third century, Pikeville has changed dramatically over the years. It is still the county seat of Pike County, and it still sits on a wide bank, at least for these hills, down the river from the place where the first county seat was established near Greasy Creek. But now the Big Sandy avoids the town altogether, and the townspeople feel no loss in its absence.

Since the Indian's grave was found, a nearby mountain was cut down and the river he swam across, the same river steamboats later plied, was moved through the Cut and the town began to forget the river ever existed. Pikeville now looks nothing like it did when Elisha and his Indian friends floated down from Greasy Creek on canoes or rafts to sell his whiskey there.

But the past has something to say to us, if we will listen, and some of us are relearning what happened in these hills so long ago. We are also beginning to appreciate what these weathered ridges mean to our souls, since the hills themselves are in peril.

Every day another mountain falls to strip mining, and even Elisha's grave is threatened, as a coal company has already obliterated most of the creek that was named for the Hopkins brothers, and the operation creeps closer to his resting place every day. He would not recognize Hopkins Creek, for no one could live there anymore. But for now, in spite of the blasting and constant drone of bulldozers, he sleeps peacefully on Ripley Knob. Beside him are three of the four women he loved, and the son who fell across his chest the night he died and who later buried him in front of the cabin the brothers built when the great trees grew huge and free, and eagles soared effortlessly from their massive branches.

He would not know Greasy Creek either, for although it has not been covered with rock and spoil like so many other places, its permutations would make it alien to what he remembered. The year after he died, the steamboats began to disappear, replaced by the railroads that were built to haul away coal the speculators bought for a fraction of the wealth they accumulated from it.

Mammy passed away on New Year's Eve 1912, and engineers stood outside her yard the day of her funeral and plotted the town they would build there. Soon the railroad came up Greasy Creek and new houses were erected, along with offices, stores, churches, a hospital, and even a brass band. The mine opened and, for a time, money flowed easily, along with strange tongues and new ways that perplexed the mountaineers. But eventually the town died too, and the immigrants moved away. Greasy Creek, having no other choice, accepted its scars and settled into isolation for decades.

When the new road is finished, the road that is churning through its heart, that seclusion will end, and the access ramp, built through the place where my people once buried their dead, will allow our children to drive away whenever they choose. And some will leave and will not return. That is the price of freedom, and we have paid it before. Greasy Creek's children have left her many times. They went away on foot, on horseback, on steamboats or trains; each new generation finding a new way to go. Later on, some left in rusty old cars with washtubs full of potatoes in their trunks, potatoes lovingly dug and washed by coal miner fathers for their factory worker sons to eat during gloomy northern winters, when food was incidental to the deeper hunger they felt for home.

When the coal company built the railroad in 1919, it took over the old Yellow Poplar narrow-gauge roadbed and expanded it, finally covering the great flat rock at the falls completely, and encroached again on the ancient pool below. It is now half the size it was when the boys of Greasy Creek swam there naked, before the War made them ashamed of each other's image. But Greasy Creek's waters, no longer drinkable, still cascade over the ancient break as if nothing has changed.

The great rock is still there somewhere, covered forever, and some of the old people say they have seen a young girl in old-fashioned clothing walking along the bank as if in search of it, or in its absence, looking for a place to sit and contemplate her sorrow. Neighbors swear they have heard children splashing there, yet find no one when they investigate. But they are not really surprised; Greasy Creek has always had its ghosts and its graves, although so many of the latter are lost. At one time, I would have demanded a stone or a mound of earth or some other proof that the people in Rissie's stories actually existed, but I have learned that is unnecessary. Although I knew no one more devoted to remembering the simple plots of almost two hundred years of my family, Rissie would have told me that all graves are ultimately lost, if I had asked her. She would have said only the spirits are eternal.

And she would have told me that if Greasy Creek is less a place today than it is a state of mind, in the grand scheme of eternity, that's probably as much as we can expect. In these hills, we have learned not to expect much more.

But I know this unreservedly: as surely as there will always be a harvest moon, there are spirits here and they are not malevolent. I know that if some of the People came to Elisha's grave a hundred years ago, or to the grave of that other warrior nearly eighty years later, they departed without a curse, for these weary hills need no more, and they left like too many of its sons and daughters, with only a backward glance, with no attempt to change what cannot be changed or turn back the clock to a time and place that no longer exists.

In these venerable hills, where the singing and laughter of giants once thundered, where phantoms still cross forgotten, sacred buffalo trails, and where eagles may yet return, we could say we are freer now than we have ever been. But in the final analysis, freedom means only that we can choose, and the Old Ones could do that. In truth, we have been given only a few more tools than they had to make our choices and control our fate.

For once again, like pilgrims in a different wilderness, we are on our own, ignorant but not stupid, unprotected but not defenseless, but finally and irrevocably left to our own devices.

Printed in the United States
59204LVS00003B/262-264